The Victors

Leslie Hardinge

Pacific Press Publishing Association
Mountain View, California
Oshawa, Ontario

Copyright © 1982 by
Pacific Press Publishing Association
Printed in United States of America

Cover by D. Tank

ISBN 0-8163-0490-4

TO
WENDY AND BRIDGET AND JOSEPH
who face the same dangers
and have the same
opportunities for
VICTORY
THIS LITTLE BOOK IS DEDICATED
with the prayer that they too
may be among those of whom
their Father will say,
THESE ARE VICTORS

Contents

Introduction

In the Scriptures the detailed records of only a few men and women of great capabilities are found. Abraham, Moses, David, Elijah, Deborah, and Ruth stand out in the Old Testament, while Paul dominates the New. But besides these individuals whose personalities and talents molded society for all time, there are many men and women whose lives affected more restricted circles, and yet whose brief histories have been recorded for our admonition and learning. And then there are hundreds of persons about whom nothing is written in the Inspired Record but their names.

Divine grace always works within the personality when human beings permit. Through the centuries the Lord has sought ways to invade the minds and experiences of individuals by His Spirit so that His designs for their lives might be worked out to the glory of His eternal kingdom, and for the greatest blessing of all concerned. While, through the centuries, the majority have refused to yield to the workings of divine grace, preferring their own ways, and thus have decided their own destinies, some have allowed God's power to mold their thinking into right decisions and strengthen their wills into virtuous actions.

The scriptural stories of the men and women who permitted the Spirit to lead them on step by step and to transform their characters into the likeness of the di-

7

vine Ideal have been left for our consideration. In the following pages thirteen biblical characters are studied. Their names are not found in the roster of the illustrious. A few of them are better known than the others. In most instances only one or two episodes of their histories have been preserved by the inspired biographer. But a careful analysis of the facts which have been recorded will reveal the clear workings of Providence which brought about the transformations in their characters. The Lord uses the circumstances of life, first to reveal the needs and weaknesses in the personality, and then He allows other happenings to teach lessons, which will aid in changing the weaknesses into strengths. For each of the individuals considered there came a moment of decision. Those who were eventually triumphant seized these decisive crises and allowed themselves to be led by God from one victory to another until Heaven's goals for their lives were reached.

In the following biographies only men and women who emerged finally victorious are studied. There are, of course, many in the sweep of the biblical narrative who failed. But the life stories we have selected emphasize only the successful, and we will seek to pinpoint the factors which led to victory. Their weaknesses are noted and then are observed being displaced by strengths. Sins are confessed and forgiven, talents are developed and used for the kingdom of God, characters are modified, and the will of God eventually is fulfilled.

Each one of these men and women has inspiring and helpful contributions to make to us today. Their problems then are our problems now, their sins are ours, and their triumphs may also be shared by us. They made decisions for God and have left us dynamic examples. They were empowered by the Spirit and point us to the Source of their strength with their encouragement that it might be ours today.

They wavered when tempted and then steadied themselves or were steadied by divine power. Their examples will infuse strength into our trembling, fluctuating lives. They chose to move into the orbit of divine grace and demonstrate that what one person has achieved in the long ago, another may also today. "There is nothing new under the sun," Solomon observed, and so the lessons they learned we may master, and what they were taught of God's will and providences they are ready to teach us.

They being dead, still speak to the twentieth century, telling us that God, who does not change, is able to do for us what He did for them. They assure us that the power which made them the victors is available for us today. They show us that the road of self-surrender and prayer, and the careful following of the Light is still the way into the holiest where are available all the resources of Omnipotence.

We shall carefully study the peculiar circumstances and conditions of their lives and characters at the time when the Spirit first introduces them to us in the salvation story. Then we shall watch as they develop under His tutelage. Thus we shall discern the ways for our own growth in knowledge and grace, and learn the power of the inspired words that the things which "were written aforetime were written for our learning" "upon whom the ends of the world are come." Romans 15:4; 1 Corinthians 10:11. These "things" in the sacred story concern the power of God to change lives into the image of His Son. We need to be admonished today, and these men and women who were victors yesteryear stand ready to admonish us day by day. Their voices call across the millennia and penetrate language barriers and cultural differences with the assurance that their God is still able to do for all of us what He did for them.

It is the prayer of the writer that the insights and satisfactions, the hope and courage, the assurance and appreciation of the divine Providences which he has seen in studying these scriptural characters, will also be supplied to each of his readers. These victorious men and women have become his helpful friends, and he takes pleasure in introducing them to all who read this little book.

Stephen—Faithful Martyr

"The blood of the martyrs is the seed of the church." I don't remember who originally said this, but whoever he was, he epitomized a profound truth. During the first decades of the Christian era three untimely and violent deaths spurred the believers to greater devotion and wider witnessing. John the Baptist was murdered in Herod's dungeon at the whim of a wanton. Jesus of Nazareth was crucified on Calvary's cross at the envy of a nation. Stephen the deacon was stoned outside Jerusalem's walls at the frustration of the Sanhedrin. The martyrdom of this first deacon proved to be one of the central dynamics in Saul's dramatic conversion and later his devoted ministry. Decades after his conversion he was haunted by this horror, Stephen's martyrdom, and often commented on its tragi-triumphant results, remembering that "when the blood of thy martyr Stephen was shed, I also was standing by, and consenting unto his death, and kept the raiment of them that slew him." Acts 22:20.

Prejudice has occasionally disrupted the cordial relationships which should exist between persons and communities. On one occasion, Miriam grew scornful of Zipporah—her brother Moses' wife—a Midianite with a complexion somewhat swarthy. The Lord showed His displeasure at this small-minded attitude by His rebuke of Miriam. See Numbers 12:1, 10, 15.

She might have picked up this attitude while growing up among Egyptians, who exhibited their "superiority" by refusing even to eat with Hebrews. Genesis 43:32. On a national scale, prejudice was the way of life in Palestine for centuries. Jesus came to break down every wall separating persons and peoples. See Ephesians 2:13, 14. In a true relationship with Him there can be "neither Jew nor Greek, there is neither bond nor free, there is neither male nor female: for ye are all one in Christ." Galatians 3:28.

But let us return to the story of Stephen and its bearing on Saul of Tarsus. Shortly after Pentecost racial jealousies wracked the Christian community. The poor Jewish members vied with the poorer Greek-speaking Jewish believers for bigger shares in the distribution of the largess of the wealthier members of the church. The apostles, sensing that their call to the gospel ministry placed them outside this kind of mundane service, set in motion a plan that was to be an important step in the future organization of the Christian church. At this time their directive to the believers read, "Look ye out among you seven men of honest report, full of the Holy Ghost and wisdom, whom we may appoint over this business." Acts 6:3. Inspiration places Stephen foremost among these seven carefully chosen deacons. He was "a man full of faith and the Holy Ghost," especially endued with "faith and power." See verses 5, 8. The immediate result of this move was equity in the distribution of commodities and peace among the believers from the two groups. This wholesome state of affairs was followed by an influx into the church of members from both the common people and the educated and influential priests in Jerusalem.

Luke records that Stephen was a "full" disciple, full of faith, full of the Spirit, and full of grace and power. His fellows freely elected him as a deacon, but God had a much more vital task awaiting him than what is often understood by this kind of ministry. He was so full that he overflowed into wider spheres of usefulness! From serving tables for the materially destitute he came to distribute the bread of life and the garments of righteousness to the poor in spirit. But nowhere is it recorded in Scripture that he relinquished his duties as a servant. He had been ordained as a deacon, and not as a minister, yet he ministered. He was not ordained as a preacher, yet he preached. He was the first lay evangelist in the history of the organized Christian church. Stephen obviously used every talent he had and God multiplied them and thus the Spirit helped him to develop others. He did not push himself into prominent positions, but his talents naturally brought him there. And although his preaching appears to have been the most effective of all the Christians at this juncture in history, none of the apostles objected or were jealous of his success. He validated the wise man's ancient observation that "a man's gift maketh room for him, and bringeth him before great men." Proverbs 18:16. And because of all these dedicated talents and loving activities he was murdered in cold blood. The shortsighted persons in the church might have wailed, "We have lost the kindest deacon and the greatest preacher and the keenest apologist we have!" But God immediately arranged that Stephen's archenemy should take his place and become the most profound theologian and most successful church developer among the early Christians.

Stephen was selected from all the Christian men in Jerusalem to be a deacon because of his lack of prejudice. It was possibly for this very reason that he was appointed head deacon to guide and influence the others. Stephen bore witness to a new spirit of Christian love and toleration.

Stephen refused to be limited by his office, but "did great wonders and miracles among the people." Acts 6:8. Stephen's contacts with the Greek-speaking Jewish Christians led him to seek occasions on which he could speak to their friends who had not yet embraced Christianity. He soon "found opportunity to preach the gospel in the synagogues of the Greek Jews. He was very active in the cause of Christ and boldly proclaimed his faith." —*The Acts of the Apostles*, p. 97. His emphasis upon the role of the Crucified stirred up considerable interest. "Learned rabbis and doctors of the law engaged in public discussion with him, confidently expecting an easy victory. But they were not able to resist the wisdom and the spirit by which he spake."—*Ibid*.

Stephen the preacher was clear and convincing. "Not only did he speak in the power of the Holy Spirit, but it was plain that he was a student of the prophecies and learned in all matters of the law. He ably defended the truths that he advocated and utterly defeated his opponents."—*Ibid*. He soon stepped, almost eagerly, into the very vortex of Christian apologetics, disputing with various factions in the synagogues. His arguments were so clear and so forceful that they proved irrefutable even to the greatest scholars among the Jews. His wisdom placed his words above controversy, and the spirit which he displayed disarmed the ill will of the open-minded. But prejudice and error do not easily yield to truth and love, and soon his enemies from among his own countrymen organized a mob, which seized him on trumped-up charges and dragged him to the Sanhedrin. By planting false ideas in the minds of the judges and by spreading various rumors which stirred up the bigoted Hebrews, they forced the high priest to demand that Stephen defend himself. Read the story in Acts 6:9-15. They then resorted to the tactic of the defeated—they hired false witnesses against him.

Long before this crisis arose Stephen might, at any moment he chose, have retired from the dangerous arena. Even while confronted by his judges, who were bent on destroying him, he could easily have recanted and thus possibly saved his life. But could he? With the love of Jesus burning in his heart, with the truth of the gospel like liquid fire upon his lips, with the longing that souls should see the way to the cross melting his spirit, and with the urgency of the task which Heaven had laid upon him driving him forward, Stephen could not turn away from his heavenly vision.

Thinking that they could easily intimidate Stephen and silence his proclamation of the gospel, the Jewish leaders pitted one of their foremost speakers against him. Saul "brought the weight of eloquence and the logic of the rabbis to bear upon the case, to convince the people that Stephen was preaching delusive and dangerous doctrines; but in Stephen he met one who had a full understanding of the purpose of God in the spreading of the gospel to other nations."—*Ibid.*, p. 98. But even before Stephen had ended his defense, his opponents, convinced that his conclusions were correct, "stopped their ears, and ran upon him with one accord, and cast him out of the city, and stoned him." Acts 7:57, 58.

Stephen's dying witness was the clarion call which gave new direction to the life of Saul of Tarsus. The learned Pharisee only dimly sensed its consquences at the time, but when he clearly heard its message, he never forgot the one whom God had used to reach his heart. With the other spectators, Saul, fascinated, watched the radiant face of Stephen, the apologist, and joined in the general acknowledgment that it appeared as the face of an angel. Acts 6:15.

An analysis of Paul's initial essay into Christian apologetics reveals the telling fact that Stephen's dying words had etched themselves indelibly into his brain. But in spite of this, or more likely because of it, Saul had agreed to Stephen's stoning, and the word he himself later used, *consenting* (Acts 8:1), reveals his inner reaction. He had virtually taken pleasure in the decision to murder the Christian deacon-apologist, and had approved of what the others had actually carried out. The root of this word translated "consenting" is found in the word used by the heavenly Father to describe His feelings for His earthborn Son, "I am well pleased." Matthew 3:17. Saul, the fanatical Pharisee, delighted at what was being inflicted upon Stephen, because he thought it benefited the cause of Hebrew nationalism. But for these sentiments Paul, the Christian apostle, had recurring and soul-tearing regrets to the day of his death.

What was this remarkable deacon-evangelist really like? The length of Stephen's ministry was totally disproportionate to the power and extent of his influence. The fruit of his life, and the results of his death, can be measured only in eternity. To find out we must first observe Stephen faithfully toiling to help the needy in days of quiet, and note how the Spirit of God possessed his spirit. We must observe the miracles he was used by Heaven to perform, and watch the infant church increase in numbers and influence because of him. And then it all suddenly ended in his arrest and arraignment before the Sanhedrin, where he found himself on trial for his life.

It was at this time that "Jesus revealed himself to Stephen while he was surrounded with pitiless foes. The martyr was given a view of the glory of God with Jesus standing at his right hand to give help to his suffering servant."—Ellen G. White, "Jesus Knocking at the Heart," *Signs*, March 3, 1890. And how did Stephen appear under pressure in the Hebrew hall of judgment? His gaze was upon the throne of God, and light from the gates of paradise shone in his eyes. His face reflected the glory which appears only on celestial countenances. And how polite and gentle were his opening remarks! His quiet, conciliatory spirit won the attention of his listeners. His speech, saturated with the true philosophy of Hebrew salvation history and warmed with the fervor of the Hebrew prophets, brought conviction to all who heard him that day. And when he made his application, his words cut through apathy and prejudice, jealousy and pride, and incised the callous casing of the hearts of his enemies. What an evangelist! How clear was the indictment, "Thou art the man!" How vividly his hearers discerned the goal of the gospel! But sinful arrogance refused to capitulate.

The word *martyr* means one who bears witness to his faith, if necessary even to the laying down of his life for what he believes. Jesus has never promised that His followers will escape the bite of the serpent, and Stephen illustrates this truth. Soon rough hands seized the gentle deacon, and coarse voices, heavy with hate and sharp with venom, clamored for his death. The bold ones dragged him from the council chamber, and the cruel ones stoned him to death, while the frustrated Saul happily cheered them on! And how did Stephen suffer? "Calling upon God, and saying, Lord Jesus, receive my spirit. And he kneeled down, and cried with a loud voice, Lord, lay not this sin to their charge. And when he had said this, he fell asleep." Acts 7:59, 60. I wonder whether Stephen had been in the crowd that had listened to the Sermon on the Mount and heard Jesus bid His followers pray for their enemies—even for their persecutors. Had he stood near the cross? Perhaps he had, but whether he had or had not, he certainly lived out this principle. One day he will realize the glorious and unexpected answer he received, when he learns in glory of the conversion of his archenemy, Saul of Tarsus.

The executioners took off their garments lest they become spotted with blood, and Saul kept them safely in his charge. But none could by this act escape Stephen's blood on their consciences. Paul the aged felt this sanguinary burden to the day of his death, although he knew he had been forgiven long before be-

17

cause of the cleansing blood of the Jesus whom Stephen proclaimed. Stephen died with his eyes fixed upon his interceding Mediator, his voice lifted to the throne in intercession for his murderers, and the commitment of his soul into the nail-pierced hands of the Master he loved. And thus "he fell asleep," a tranquil and quiet final resting. "In the world . . . tribulation" (John 16:33), but in his heart he had the peace that passes understanding.

Stephen testified to the reality of the life beyond this life with Jesus and the angels. His vision robbed the terror from his dying, and because of his death we learn that martydom is sometimes necessary for the conversion of a soul. By Stephen's murder Saul became Paul, and the Christian church incurred a debt it will never be able to repay. His loving prayer echoes across the chasms of dark ignorance and sharp bigotry, "Lord, lay not this sin to their charge," and moves our hearts today.

Lydia—Businesswoman

Lydia, the first person to accept Christianity in Europe, was not a European! She was an Asian whose hometown was Thyatira, a garrison city by the river Lycus in the province of Lydia in Asia Minor. Acts 16:14. Thyatira was one of the seven churches to which Christ directed a warning epistle. Read Revelation 2:18-29. It might have been because of her place of origin that Lydia was given her name. Perhaps adverse conditions among the believers in Thyatira caused Lydia to move to an environment more conducive to her becoming a Christian.

Thyatira was famous not only for producing a purple dye, but also for fabrics which were woven in that city and then dyed. This cloth, popular in the Roman world, was used to make the loose robe called the toga. It might have been to better her business that the enterprising Lydia decided to travel to Philippi to open up new markets for her products. The term Luke used indicates that she dealt in first-class goods. She must therefore have had adequate capital to be able to trade in such articles. See William Ramsay, *St. Paul the Traveller and Roman Citizen*, p. 214. All things worked together for the good of Lydia and Europe.

When her story opens in Scripture, Lydia had evidently gained some financial success. Luke noted in passing that she owned a home large enough to accommodate Paul's entire missionary company. Acts 16:15. As Inspiration is silent regarding her husband, she might well have been widowed. Let us study the few details given to us concerning the life of this traveled and successful businesswoman who chose to locate and conduct her business in a foreign land.

The Lord had already set in motion the train of events which eventually brought about dramatic changes in Lydia's life. Before He gave Paul his dream of a benighted Europe, God was providing for the needs of those who would be making "the Macedonian call" for help. Long ago a scenario something like this was suggested by William Ramsay. Paul, frustrated in his evangelism in Asia by the Spirit's intervention (Acts 16:6, 7), arrived tired and sick at Troas. There he consulted Dr. Luke, who then accepted the gospel. Luke the Macedonian invited Paul to take the good news to his kindred. That night in a prophetic dream Paul saw a "certain" Macedonian (Luke's expression indicates a person well-known to him), calling for help. Was this visionary European Luke himself? It is possible. I like the idea. Following this vision, with Luke as his guide, Paul and Silas immediately set sail from Troas in Asia for Europe. Disembarking at the port of Neapolis, the travelers went on to Philippi, a Roman colonial center and the most influential city in that area. Acts 16:11, 12.

Wondering how and where to begin his evangelizing efforts, Paul almost immediately heard of a company of women who were said to "worship God," and decided that these proselytes were prime prospects for discipling. On the first Sabbath after their arrival the missionaries set out to find them. When they had located their meeting place, they "sat down, and spake unto the women which resorted thither." Acts 16:13. Luke's expression "worshipped God" is a Hebraism suggesting that these women had accepted the God of the Jews and were complying with the requirements of the Old Testament. With Lydia as their leader, they grew to be persons of regular and habitual prayer (Acts 16:13), as well as keen students of the Scriptures.

Josephus recorded that Seleucus I was very favorable to the Jews and granted them the citizenship of Thyatira, a city which he founded.—Josephus *Antiquities* 12:3. This freedom of worship and full rights as citizens made it easier for pagans to accept Judaism. Lydia had evidently become a proselyte in Thyatira, and from thence had carried her faith to Europe. Since there was apparently no synagogue in Philippi, she found other kindred souls interested in the Scriptures, and together they discovered a secluded spot in which to meet outside the city on the bank of the stream Gangites.

Lydia was obviously the leader of this Sabbath prayer and study circle whose aim was to seek for scriptural truth. It is vital to note that her journey into Christianity consisted of two stages. As the direct result of her compliance with the light she had already received as a proselyte to Judaism, Lydia was led by the Spirit to the place where she was able to gain fuller light and deeper insights into the will of God. Had she refused to take her stand first for the partial truth held by the Jews, she would not have been given the opportunity to take the next step into the full light of the gospel of Jesus Christ.

Paul immediately began to explain to this group the message of salvation contained in the Scriptures. Lydia listened intently. The historian's construction "attended unto" indicates that hers was a continuing listening. The phrase suggests that she gave her whole mind to the ideas being presented. And the Lord, who had awakened her interest in the gospel in the first place, "opened" her heart fully (Acts 16:14) to receive its message in all its power. Luke's word *opened* is also used to describe the opening of the womb in conception (Luke 2:23), the ears of the deaf

21

(Mark 7:34, 35), the eyes of the blind (Luke 24:31) to restored functioning, the Scriptures to those who were confused (Luke 24:32), and here, the heart of yearning souls to richest comprehension (Acts 16:14). Luke also employed this word to tell us how Jesus, following His walk to Emmaus, induced His followers in the upper room to understand the message concerning His resurrection and its consequences. Luke 24:45. The root of this term suggests the removal of the lid of a box (Matthew 2:11), as illustrated by the wise men who opened up the containers of their treasures for the Boy Jesus. It also describes the opening of the doors of our hearts to receive the knocking Christ into our lives. Revelation 3:20. What a preacher Paul must have been, and what a listener Lydia certainly was!

Throughout the time of her indoctrination, Lydia's part was the maintaining of a careful and continual attention to the preaching of Paul, while the Spirit's part was that of opening her heart to comprehend the message more perfectly. In scriptural imagery *heart* describes the mental faculties of the disciples which decide and act. Ellen G. White long ago observed, "We must have more than an intellectual belief in the truth. Many of the Jews were convinced that Jesus was the Son of God, but they were too proud and ambitious to surrender. They decided to resist the truth, and they maintained their opposition. They did not receive into the heart the truth as it is in Jesus. When the truth is held as truth only by the conscience, when the heart is not stimulated and made receptive, only the mind is affected. But when the truth is received as truth by the heart, it has passed through the conscience, and has captivated the soul with its pure principles. It is placed in the heart by the Holy Spirit, who reveals its beauty to the mind, that its transforming power may be seen in the character."—*Evangelism*, p. 291.

Luke's term *attended* (Acts 16:14), describing Lydia's reaction to Paul's appeal, is a picturesque one.

Outside the Scriptures it depicts the alert way in which a captain maintains the steady course of his ship until it reaches its haven. And so the word came to mean embracing ideas being explained or yielding assent. The Lord's aim was that Lydia should understand the concepts presented by Paul and the practical lessons he taught.

She eventually understood the objectives of his preaching and then willingly allowed her life to be steered toward them. Lydia was clear in her thinking and prompt in acting, seeking only God's ideal for her life with an open, eager mind. It was because of these traits that she became an influential charter member of the first European church.

With her household Lydia was soon baptized. Acts 16:15. This is the first time a baptism is mentioned in connection with Paul's evangelism, and Luke must have intended to call attention to this first European baptismal service. In this story we also find reference to the first Christian household. When groups of closely knit persons accept the message of God, they strengthen one another. To show her appreciation for the gift of eternal life which had been presented to her by the evangelists, Lydia made an earnest appeal to them, which must have gone something like this: If your estimate of my faithfulness still stands (the perfect tense of *judged* is used by Luke), please come and stay as guests in my home as long as you like (the author used the present continuous tense of *abide*).

Luke recorded that Lydia not only "besought" them to accept her offer, but that she also actually "constrained" them. Acts 16:15. Initially Paul was evidently a little uncertain as to whether he should accept her invitation, but allowed himself to be overborne by her persuasive pressures. Outside the New Testament this word, rendered "constrained," is used to describe the result of the employment of force or even violence! In the Scripture it speaks of compelling by overmuch entreaty. Cf. Luke 24:29. The generous, hospitable, and friendly Lydia refused to take No for an answer when she offered her home and hospitality to the missionaries!

Not long after this, "as we went to prayer" (Acts 16:16), Luke remembered Paul and Silas were hindered in their work by false testimony from masters of a devil-possessed young woman from whom they had exorcised the evil spirit. This girl had practiced as a medium, and now her masters, having been financially reduced, decided to precipitate a riot against the missionaries. Acts 16:16-20. The apostles were arrested and scourged on orders from the magistrates, and then summarily imprisoned. From jail the singing evangelists were rescued by a heaven-sent earthquake. Acts 16:21-26. When the whole sorry yet triumphant affair ended, "they went out of the prison, and entered into the house of Lydia." Acts 16:40. And what a reception they must have received! Lydia might have argued that her association with the unpopular missionaries might adversely affect her business and so left them alone. But she had only thoughts of befriending her benefactors, at any cost to herself. When they had washed and taken care of their wounds, Lydia gave them food. After they had eaten and rested for a while, Paul and Silas "comforted" or "exhorted" the frightened and frustrated believers, and shortly after set forth for further missionary enterprises. We never read of Lydia by name after this act of generous and kindly hospitality. Inspiration evidently wishes us to concentrate only on the episodes presented in the New Testament.

The Lord is wondrously encouraging to His messengers. In Thessalonica Paul would again be persecuted, and in Athens he was shortly to meet with cynicism and intellectual pride. His life would be threatened and his words ridiculed, and he himself despised, while only "Dionysius the Areopagite, and a woman named Demaris," and some others (Acts 17:34) would accept his message. But through his experience in Philippi, Providence had fortified him for the rejection and frustration which lay ahead. His enthusiasm would be bolstered in the Greek capital as he remembered Lydia's faithfulness to the gospel and her kindness both to him and his companions. In this way he would be strengthened to realize anew that God has His lovely jewels in every place.

An important way in which God prepares souls for the kingdom of heaven is also revealed in this simple yet condensed narrative. Let us review the details. Lydia, an immigrant to Europe, came from a well-known town in another country. Those of us who have migrated have some idea of the forces and factors which must have induced her to sever her home ties. We understand, too, how her mind would be open to new ideas and new people in a new culture and in a new environment. Somewhere along the way she had met with Jews and had learned to respect their religion and to worship their God. Then in the land of her adoption she had come across other kindred spirits, and together these women had decided regularly to spend the sacred Sabbath hours at a secluded spot by the river in the study of the Hebrew Scriptures and in prayer.

When Paul and Silas arrived at Philippi, directed there in a dream, the time was right as far as the experiences and spiritual development of these women were concerned. And so the Lord caused the paths of the two parties to converge. Thus through the outworking of all these circumstances, Paul and Lydia met briefly, and a candle was lighted in Philippi which was eventually to illumine the whole of Europe. Almost immediately after Lydia's baptism, Paul and Silas were speeded on their way by seemingly adverse forces, and so the work of discipling continued in Thessalonica and other areas of Europe. But Lydia had been sealed as a child of God by her short encounter with the Christian missionaries, and the Spirit had accomplished His plan for her life.

Today, too, for one soul, for a single household, Heaven is prepared to work long years with untiring effort. And into this divine scheme God calls for the assistance of His servants. Each one has his special part to play, and according to the faithfulness with which each fulfills his mission, the kingdom of heaven is advanced. God still has his openhearted, eager, would-be disciples everywhere, thirsting for light and hope, and it is the privilege of His workers to be responsive to the Spirit's call and to be present where they are needed because of their special talents. When souls are prepared for a further stage of enlightenment and are ready to take the next step in their walk to the gates of pearl, these witnesses of the gospel are to be present to testify to them concerning the "way, the truth, and the life." The helpers of the openhearted, eager Lydias in every age and in every community, are the Pauls and Paulas who are not disobedient to their heavenly vision.

With Lydia to encourage the believers in Philippi, the church in that city flourished. Paul often recalled his various experiences in the ministry. As he sat in his dungeon cell, he was warmed by the love and concern of this most solicitous group of Philippian Christians to whom he had witnessed in person and by messenger and through prayer during his life of service. The Philippians had assisted Paul in every way they could, much more generously than had any other church which he had pastored. And the rejoicing which they brought to him he embedded in the epistle of joy which he wrote to them.

Lydia, the Asian widow who progressed through her conversion to Judaism to become the first Christian in Europe and the charter member and leader of the church at Philippi—the successful, openhearted, generous, career woman—must have played a compelling

26

part in these living services to her beloved mentor. Is it possible that Paul was referring to her in his pastoral message as his "yokefellow" (feminine in Greek, and therefore indicating a woman)? No one knows for certain, but he certainly might have been. "I entreat thee also, true yokefellow, help these women which laboured with me in the gospel." Philippians 4:3. He knew that she would still be helping "those women," other widows, to fulfill their responsibilities in the gospel. What pleasant memories Lydia evoked in her erstwhile pastor's mind during his last days on earth! And what a comfort these memories proved to be. And what an example she set all Christians in every age to help those whom the Spirit has brought within the circle of their lives and who have guided them to understand the gospel. Lydia's kindly, happy spirit pervades the letter Paul wrote to her friends and to her, in the first church in Europe, and lifts our hearts heavenward today.

Onesiphorus—Pastor's Helper

Paul mentioned Onesiphorus (pronounced Oh-nee-sif'-erus) twice in his letter to Timothy. Reading between the lines, we conclude that Onesiphorus had probably been converted to Christianity during the three years of ministry in which the apostle preached in Ephesus. Acts 19:1-41; 20:1. Onesiphorus had eventually been appointed an elder of the church in that city. Paul later called for the elders of the church in Ephesus to meet him for his farewell address at Miletus. Acts 20:17. There he had reminded them of his ministry carried on in "all seasons." Acts 20:18. The apostle then called upon Onesiphorus and the others to "take heed" personally and pastorally to the instructions from heaven (Acts 20:28-31), and then commended them to the keeping of God (Acts 20:32-35). As their beloved pastor bade them farewell, Onesiphorus must have been with the group of church officers in weeping "sore" and falling on Paul's neck and kissing him good-bye. They were especially moved by the implications of his words that they would see his face no more. Acts 20:36-38.

Years later, while Paul languished in a Roman prison under the death sentence of Caesar, he remembered his friends from Asia with the greatest affection. The executioner's sword was pointing out Paul's immediate path, and in the somber reflection of that bloody sword he thought of Onesiphorus and his family. In his letter to Timothy, Paul mentioned Onesiphorus and his family in company with his dear friends Priscilla and Aquila. Although Onesiphorus was not numbered among the learned or exalted whom Paul had met, his niche in the apostle's heart was warm and enduring. As his pastor, Paul had come to love and appreciate him dearly.

I can almost see Paul in the dank and dismal dungeon of the tyrant Nero daily awaiting the signal to be marched out to die. All the relatives and friends of a man condemned to death by Caesar were in mortal jeopardy of being executed with him. Their lives depended on the whim of Nero. This slaughter of innocent members of the family or even acquaintances happened on many occasions.

Only the most devoted and loving would risk exposure by associating with Paul and thus show that they were the friends of one already condemned. Because of this constant danger of being arrested and beheaded together with Paul, many Christians had abandoned him. The apostle noted with sadness and regret, "Demas hath fosaken me, having loved this present world." 2 Timothy 4:10. He also stated that all his friends from Asia who had happened to be in Rome had turned away from him (2 Timothy 1:15), fearful of the consequences of being associated with one who had incurred the hatred of Nero—See Eusebius *Ecclesiastical History* 2. 22. Later in his epistle Paul reminded Timothy that "at my first answer no man stood with me, but all men forsook me." 2 Timothy 4:16. This was his initial defense after his second imprisonment in Rome. "Stood with me" literally means that no professional or friendly advocate had risked his life and reputation, and come forward as his defender and companion. Then Paul revealed his real feelings, "I pray God that it may not be laid to their charge. Notwithstanding the Lord stood with me, and strengthened me." Verses 16, 17. Paul does not appeal to Timothy out and out to come to him, but hints that he would like to have Timothy's presence and support in his serious conditon. 2 Timothy 4:21. His invocation for those who had forsaken him carries echoes of Stephen's prayer for his persecutors to which Paul had listened more than thirty years before. Acts 7:60.

One day as he was languishing in the Mamertine prison, I like to imagine that a face appeared at the opening in the ceiling of his cell, and a familiar voice called out, "Hail! is Paul of Tarsus in there?" I can almost hear the excited greetings, the eager questions tripping over each other regarding old friends and conditions in Ephesus, and then, all too quickly, Onesiphorus was gone with the promise that he would return as soon as possible.

As Paul retold his experience to Timothy, his beloved son in the faith, he prayed, "The Lord give mercy unto the house of Onesiphorus." 2 Timothy 1:16. And then he reminded the young pastor why the loving face of Onesiphorus sprang to life in his memory. "For he oft refreshed me, and was not ashamed of my chain: but, when he was in Rome, he sought me out very diligently, and found me." 2 Timothy 1:16, 17. And for the second time the apostle prayed, "The Lord grant unto him that he may find mercy of the Lord in that day: and in how many things he ministered unto me at Ephesus, thou knowest very well." 2 Timothy 1:18. How I would love my friends to remember me in this way! From Paul's term *ministered*, derived from the same root from which *deacon* springs and which means to supply the wants of the needy, some have concluded that Onesiphorus was an elder or minor minister in the Ephesian church. This is probable. But in this passage the apostle appears to have been speaking of more personal services which had been rendered to him by Onesiphorus.

When Onesiphorus and his family yielded their hearts to the gospel's power, they opened their hearts to the homeless apostle. Then Paul reminded Timothy, "In how many things he ministered unto me at Ephesus, thou knowest very well." Nothing was too much for Onesiphorus and his family to do for their pastor Paul. They had stayed awake at night thinking of the "many things" they might do for their beloved mentor!

And then Paul recollected for Timothy his difficult experiences in Rome during his trial, concluding with the words, "All they which are in Asia be turned away from me." 2 Timothy 1:15. His onetime friends had disappeared, terrified by the danger they imagined they were in. But then the apostle remembered that *all* was probably too wide a term. He readily called to mind the one from Asia who had not forgotten him! He could see in his mind's eye the smiling face of Onesiphorus and could hear again his own involuntary question when he had first been visited by him. "Onesiphorus, how did you get here?" May I reconstruct his reply? "It wasn't easy, pastor. I've been looking for you all over the city, and have only just found you." As Paul told Timothy this story he used the words, "When he was in Rome, he sought me out very diligently, and found me." Verse 17. Can you get the picture? "Very diligently" or "with extraordinary diligence," he "sought me out" or "kept up his quest" until "he found me." I like that, and I like Onesiphorus for that. Many of the persons whom he asked concerning the whereabouts of the condemned prisoner probably felt that they might be associated with Paul, if they acknowledged that they even knew where he was. But Onesiphorus was persistent, and his love and loyalty and friendship were eventually rewarded. One day he discovered his beloved Paul again in jail!

And while he was in Rome, Onesiphorus came "often" to visit Paul, who described his activities as "refreshing" to his soul. How oft he "refreshed me" are Paul's words to Timothy. This phrase suggests a lifting of the spirits, a warming at the flame of love, through a word of appreciation and encouragement. When the world seemed to be against Paul, his soul soared in joy and praise at the coming of his friend. Such is the power of true friendship spilling over into acts of gentle hospitality. The apostle recollected that "he oft refreshed me, and was not ashamed of my chain." In spite of the possibility of danger of confiscation of property and even death, and ever-present personal ridicule and humiliation, Onesiphorus had not missed a single opportunity to do all in his power during his stay at Rome to "refresh" Paul.

The apostle's word *refresh* is found in the New Testament only in this passage. But it is illuminated by usages in the Septuagint. Here are some examples. Through the provisions of the Sabbath law even oxen and servants were to "be refreshed." Exodus 23:12. In another context the troubled demonic spirit of Saul was "refreshed" by David's playing soothingly upon his harp. 1 Samuel 16:23. Later in life David himself, seared by the curses of Shimei, was "refreshed" by the Holy Spirit as a result of his prayers and meditation upon the goodness and care of the Lord. 2 Samuel 16:14. Perhaps the most revealing use of this word by the psalmist is in the rendering "to put on a bright face," or in the language of the Revised Version, "O spare me that I may *brighten* up." Psalm 39:13, marginal reading. What a lovely picture! One look at the face of Onesiphorus, and Paul's outlook on life brightened up. The presence of the elder of Ephesus chased the shadows from his pastor's cell. And this did not happen only once, Onesiphorus *often* brightened things up, the apostle noted! What a precious friend! And even today the face of Onesiphorus smiles across the centuries, encouraging, refreshing, adding a lift to life's song and a firmness to the step. Centuries ago

Onesiphorus made the pathway of Paul into the dark unknown less dark by being near him. And as we remember him today he does the same for us.

In some churches the pastor finds himself in a state somewhat like that of the apostle. His heart cries out "all . . . have forsaken me!" He feels so alone. Where are all his friends? Where are those who yesteryear crowded about him and hung on his every word? "Having loved the world," they are gone just when he needs them most. But thank God Onesiphorus is not dead! Even though we last met him in Ephesus, he is in every congregation. He senses that his pastor needs help, and often comes to find him and brighten him up!

Paul looked forward to "that day" when all the good that Onesiphorus had done would be remembered by the eternal Judge. Henri Daniel-Rops, in his *Daily Life in the Time of Jesus,* page 397, pointed out that "the Day of Atonement, *Yom Kippur,* was so important that if a man spoke simply of 'the day,' everyone knew that he meant this particular day." The apostle Paul, in his letter to the Hebrews used this expression again. See Hebrews 10:25. Almost a century ago B. F. Westcott pointed out that when Paul spoke of "the day approaching" he had the Day of Atonement in mind.— *Hebrews* (London, 1889), p. 281. The apostle then went on to talk of the subsequent second advent. See Hebrews 10:36-39. In the antitypical day of atonement, during the judgment which makes "inquisition" (Psalm 9:12) into all the sins of God's people, the true worth of human life will be revealed. Paul well knew that Onesiphorus and his family would pass the audit with colors flying!

There will be many surprises on that judgment day. The cry of the good, and the wail of the bad will alike be, "When—Lord—?" On that illuminating day, many will reverse their values. Estimates we may have had of persons will need to be revised. Evaluations of services will then need to be remade. On that joyous

33

day all the obscure Onesiphoruses will come into their own! On earth they have almost anonymously moved from one despondent soul to another, brightening things up for them. But in the radiance of God's eternal day their love and simple serving, their understanding of human need, and their readiness to do their part to meet that need will be more valuable than the gold of Ophir.

Hannah—Pious Wife and Mother

We might never have heard of Hannah had she not been childless. Her son Samuel, whom she later bore, probably wrote her biography. As he introduces his mother to us, he stresses the raging conflict in her home. Because she and her husband had no child, Elkanah suspected she was barren. He then decided to bring another woman into his household by whom he might have a family. While polygamy is not explicitly condemned in the Scriptures, there is no instance recorded in which a polygamous home was happy and successful. Complications and conflicts in the household relationship produced nothing but trouble for all the persons concerned and also multiplied problems for many generations yet to be born. Polygamy in Elkanah's home was no exception.

Peninnah, the new wife, soon had a flourishing family, and this aroused in her heart feelings of superiority and arrogance. She felt that she was obviously favored of God, and rationalized that Hannah was suffering under a divine curse. This narrow-minded opinion made her both proud and insolent.

"Elkanah faithfully observed the ordinances of God. The worship at Shiloh was still maintained, but on account of irregularities in the ministration his services were not required at the sanctuary, to which, being a Levite, he was to give attendance. Yet he went up with

35

his family to worship and sacrifice at the appointed gatherings.''—*Patriarchs and Prophets*, p. 569.

As was customary during the festivities connected with the sanctuary services, Elkanah gave gifts to each member of his household, but to Hannah, his beloved and favorite wife, he gave a double portion. This aroused Peninnah's jealousy even more. She demanded similar treatment, and "taunted Hannah with her childless state as evidence of the Lord's displeasure. This was repeated from year to year, until Hannah could endure it no longer. Unable to hide her grief, she wept without restraint, and withdrew from the feast. Her husband vainly sought to comfort her. 'Why weepest thou? and why eatest thou not? and why is thy heart grieved?' he said; and 'am I not better to thee than ten sons?' ''—*Ibid.*, p. 570. Hannah uttered no reproaches, nor did she in any way encourage a contest for position.

"The burden which she could share with no earthly friend she cast upon God. Earnestly she pleaded that He would take away her reproach and grant her the precious gift of a son to nurture and train for Him. And she made a solemn vow that if her request were granted, she would dedicate her child to God, even from its birth."—*Ibid.*

"And it came to pass, as she continued praying before the Lord, that Eli marked her mouth. Now Hannah, she spake in her heart; only her lips moved, but her voice was not heard: therefore Eli thought she had been drunken." 1 Samuel 1:12, 13. To what a degraded state the general worshipers in Israel had evidently come! For the high priest unquestioningly to suspect drunkenness in one who prayed fervently even in the sanctuary is appalling!

But Hannah quietly replied, "No, my lord, I am a woman of a sorrowful spirit: I have drunk neither wine nor strong drink, but have poured out my soul before the Lord. Count not thine handmaid for a daughter of

Belial: for out of the abundance of my complaint and grief have I spoken hitherto." 1 Samuel 1:15, 16.

The high priest, with all his failings, was yet a man of God, and he was deeply affected by her gentle response. His heart melted with the rebuke he had received from her, and he uttered a blessing: "Go in peace: and the God of Israel grant thee thy petition that thou hast asked of him." In process of time Hannah's boon was granted, and in joy she named her son Samuel, "Asked of God." And now she poured upon the boy all the love of her heart. "Day by day, as she watched his expanding powers and listened to his childish prattle, her affections entwined about him more closely. He was her only son, the special gift of Heaven; but she had received him as a treasure consecrated to God, and she would not withhold from the Giver His own."—*Ibid.*, pp. 570, 571. Ellen White says, "During the first three years of the life of Samuel the prophet, his mother carefully taught him to distinguish between good and evil."—*S.D.A. Bible Commentary*, vol. 2, p. 1008. After his third birthday she accompanied her husband and the rest of the family to Shiloh, and presented her precious gift to Eli. "O my lord, . . . I am the woman that stood by thee here, praying unto the Lord. For this child I prayed; and the Lord hath given me my petition. . . . Therefore also I have lent him unto the Lord." 1 Samuel 1:26-28.

Hannah stands among the most devoted mothers of Scripture, and the gift of her son to God is comparable with Abraham's sacrifice of Isaac. She knew of the sorry conditions in the home of Eli. She was aware of the depravity of his sons and of the inquity which the high priest's overindulgence had produced in circles far afield from his own home. But in spite of her knowledge, she fulfilled her vow and gave her boy to the Lord to be educated in the keeping of the aging priest. She was a woman of her word, for what she promised she carried out to the best of her ability and without delay, cost her what it might.

After presenting her son to Eli, Hannah was granted the gift of prophecy by the Lord and immediately poured forth her heart in grateful adoration to God. Years later her son Samuel, also endowed with the gift of inspiration, incorporated his mother's poem into the canon of Scriptures. 1 Samuel 2:1-10. As Hannah expressed her gratitude for the Lord's past blessings, she was led to declare, with the utmost confidence, her trust in His future watchcare of her family and His people.

Hannah remembered the insolent words spoken by Peninnah, and gave this advice: "Talk no more so exceeding proudly; let not arrogancy come out of your mouth: for so the Lord is a God of knowledge, and by him actions are weighed." 1 Samuel 2:3. She then sang of the goodness of God in vindicating the cause of the righteous and uplifting those who were cast down. "Hannah's words were prophetic, both of David, who should reign as king of Israel, and of the Messiah, the Lord's Annointed. . . . The song points to the destruction of the enemies of God and the final triumph of His redeemed people."—*Patriarchs and Prophets,* p. 572.

Hannah's quiet spirit and gentle conduct is shown in stark relief against the backdrop of the worldly sophistication and cruelty of Peninnah. Hannah's submission to God and her trust in His providence led her to give her son to her nation as a gift that blessed many generations. Through Samuel's service to his king and people and by the exercise of his prophetic gift to glorify his God, he reached a position in history attained by but few.

Hannah was one of the most effective mothers in history. Although she had her son in her care for only three years, this brief period was sufficient for her to lay a foundation that formed a character which elevated Samuel to a position among the greatest men of history. From his earliest days she had taught her son to love and reverence God, and she had constantly told Him he belonged to God. It seems almost incredible that Hannah succeeded in planting these ideas in a mind only three years old! At an age when most infants are allowed to gaze by the hour at TV, Hannah succeeded in training her infant son to make decisions which lasted into eternity. "His early training led him to choose to maintain his Christian integrity. What a reward was Hannah's! and what an encouragement to faithfulness is her example!"—Ellen G. White, *Review and Herald*, Sept. 8, 1904.

Year by year Hannah returned to Shiloh to see her growing child. "Every day he was the subject of her prayers. Every year she made, with her own hands, a robe of service for him; and as she went up with her husband to worship at Shiloh, she gave the child this reminder of her love. Every fiber of the little garment had been woven with a prayer that he might be pure, noble, and true. She did not ask for her son worldly greatness, but she earnestly pleaded that he might attain that greatness which Heaven values—that he might honor God and bless his fellow men."—*Patriarchs and Prophets*, p. 572. Samuel never forgot the influence of his godly mother.

Hannah did not ask God for worldly honor for her son. All she wished for him was that he might serve his Lord with honor and faithfulness and his fellowmen with integrity and kindness. Samuel's ministry as judge and kingmaker was most influential in the history of Israel at a crucial time. Without his steady hand, the Hebrew nation might have been plunged into civil war and anarchy, and fallen prey to enemies marshaled at its borders. He helped to reverse the tendency of the later judges and paved the way for the reign of David and Solomon.

Samuel's firsthand knowledge of the failure of parental training in the home of Eli led him to establish the schools of the prophets to counteract this evil. He was the first organizer of Christian education, and in his schools he taught the principles which had been instilled into his mind by his mother. Through this means he helped to stem the tide of apostasy.

Long dead, this faithful woman Hannah, kind and true, full of prayer and devotion to God, uncomplaining and trustful, became in fact "the mother of Israel." And Hannah's influence, through the life and writings of her son, still blesses mankind.

Onesimus—Runaway Slave

We would never have heard of Onesimus had he not run away, and he ran away because he was a slave. During New Testament times slavery was an important part of the social and economic life of the Roman world. Large masses of men and women, perhaps sixty million altogether, worked as slaves in every part of the empire! But lest we should think of all slaves as menial and illiterate we should remember that among them were physicians and teachers, artists and lawyers, as well as numbers of almost every other profession and craft. By accident of birth, through problems caused by war or debt, a man or a woman might be forced into slavery, and then it cost a great deal of money (see Acts 22:28) to emerge from this segment of society into that of freeman and freewoman. Onesimus toiled for his master Philemon day after day, and longed, as every slave does, for emancipation.

One day, probably after years of dreaming and months of planning, Onesimus disappeared, leaving his jobs unfinished and his room empty. He had absconded to find freedom and fortune in distant lands and to make a new and independent life for himself. Years later, when writing to Philemon about Onesimus, Paul hinted that he would assume any indebtedness which the slave might have incurred. Philemon 18, 19. Onesimus had probably purloined from his owner what he could carry away easily, and had escaped into the big, wide world to make a new life for himself, leaving his master Philemon disappointed, angry, and frustrated.

Where Onesimus traveled and how he managed to eke out a living we are not told, but his conscience must have weighed heavily every day. As he bought provisions in the marketplaces he must have eyed every face nervously, terrified that he would be recognized and reported to the authorities. This would have meant only one thing—he would be taken back to his master under guard and exposed to the penalties of the law and the rigors of an unknown future, should his master press charges.

Eventually, Onesimus arrived in Rome, unscathed and undetected, for all intents and purposes, a free man. He must have thought that in the large metropolis, with multitudes from the provinces coming and going, few questions would be asked of an unobtrusive stranger, as everybody seemed to be a stranger! Here he must have relaxed more and more as the days went by, finding a niche for himself in society, but never far away from his haunting conscience often quickened to remorse by memories of home and his kind master and his own evil deeds.

By the time Onesimus arrived in Rome, the apostle Paul had also reached the capitol, but he was a prisoner in bonds awaiting trial for his faith with a conscience free in the Lord. He could look all men in the face unafraid. At the beginning of his stay, Paul was permitted to live in his own hired house in the charge of a soldier, who was probably chained to him continuously. But Paul was free to visit his friends, to have them visit him, and to share the gospel of the Lord Jesus Christ with anyone who chose to listen to his message. Among the crowds of those who came to listen to Paul's preaching was Onesimus. Although we are left in the dark as to why he came at all, we may be certain that thoughts of his Christian master and the stories Paul told about Jesus which he must have heard in days long past in Colossae must have moved him to attend Paul's preaching services. With an interest quickened by the Spirit, he was mysteriously impelled toward the apostle about whom he had probably heard often enough as the evangelist who had won his master for the Lord.

By this time Paul was an experienced evangelist and a powerful soul winner. His burning words had set many hearts aflame for the Lord Jesus Christ in many cities. And now in Rome his influence was felt even within Caesar's household. See Philippians 4:27. Paul's Spirit-indicted messages changed the life and outlook of Onesimus, and he soon became a thoroughly converted Christian. I like to imagine that he then came with his problems to his new pastor. What was he to do? he must have inquired, after confessing to him that he was a runaway slave, and to make it worse, that he had robbed his master, and thus stood in double jeopardy. And as they talked, the whole sordid story must slowly have emerged, or perhaps been blurted out.

As all good pastors do, Paul must have listened patiently and attentively, with an impassive yet concerned countenance and with a sympathetic manner. He must have observed with deep satisfaction the convicting, re-creating power of grace working through the invisible ministry of the Spirit in the thinking of Onesimus. He knew that his words had merely been the catalyst used by Heaven to move the runaway robber toward the cross. Under his gaze a child of Christ was being born! I can almost hear Paul's words as he slowly began to direct the mind and heart of the penitent slave to face what he must have already half admitted to himself. Onesimus must make his relationships right with God and with his master Philemon, and accept whatever consequences were due to him. Scripture passages must have been carefully studied, earnest prayers lifted to the throne of grace, and confession and renunciation come about. Then came the resolution to restore what he owed and to carry his repentance and confession back to Colossae. I imagine that there were tears of remorse and sighs of regret, and then as Onesimus made up his mind to follow the leadings of the Spirit wherever they might point and to accept whatever the consequences might be, the peace that passes understanding flooded his soul.

Paul had probably already begun his Epistle to the Colossians before he met his new convert from that city. He might easily have added a sentence or two commending Onesimus to Philemon and soliciting the fellowship and forgiveness of the church members on his behalf. But he decided instead to write a personal letter to Philemon. Unlike his other epistles, this one did not deal with various aspects of the ministry or with questions of theology. It was simply a gentle heart-to-heart appeal to an injured master on behalf of a fugitive slave who was now a repentant sinner and a born-again Christian. In the weeks since they had first met, a bond of love had been forged between the pastor and the young disciple, whom he called affectionately, "my son Onesimus whom I have begotten in my bonds." Philemon 10. And because of this, Paul could write to Philemon, "I am sending him back to you, sending my very heart." Philemon 12, RSV.

And now the events in the lives of the various characters had almost gone full cycle in this quiet drama. Paul had known Philemon very closely. Although there is no record that he had met any of his servants in Colossae, Paul had been used to bring Philemon's erstwhile slave to Christ in faraway Rome and to direct his way back to Colossae and his master. His letter was to be the vital link in what he hoped would be an act of total reconciliation. I can imagine Onesimus and his newfound friend Tychicus setting out on the journey from Italy to Asia with Paul's three precious epistles, those to the churches of Ephesus and Colossae and his personal note to Philemon. Traveling by land and sea, facing the rigors and hardships of the way, the couriers eventually arrived at Ephesus and were given a joyous welcome by the members of the Christian community in that city. The Epistle to the Ephesians must then have been read, and Tychicus must have shared with the eager believers his personal reminiscences of Paul and collected news to take back to the apostle. And then the way of the two couriers beckoned on to Colossae, and for Onesimus the fear of his encounter with his outraged master and an uncertain future. But I like to think that all along the road the two men prayed earnestly that the Lord, who had so far led and blessed him, would continue to direct the journey through life of the runaway. I imagine that Onesimus had very mixed feelings as he neared the familiar sights and sounds and smells of his home territory. And then at last they were at Colossae and the home of Philemon, who was eagerly reading Paul's letter.

After the initial surprise and joy of the meeting, Onesimus must have looked away from the searching eyes of his master, ashamed and downcast. I can almost hear the voice of the runaway slave sobbing words something like these, "I have sinned against heaven and in thy sight. And am no more worthy to be called thy slave. Do to me what seemeth good." Cf. Luke 15:17-19. And I can almost see the arms of Philemon thrown about the shoulders of the young man (cf. Luke 15:20), as tears of joy were shed and words of forgiveness spoken. And so in the mystery of the kingdom of God a runaway slave became a brother beloved. Paul had appreciated Onesimus's helpfulness in Rome, and had hinted to Philemon that he might wish to set his slave at liberty so that Onesimus could rejoin the aged Paul's company. But we are told nothing of the effects on the two men of Paul's letter and so are left to wonder.

As the only personal letter in the New Testament, save perhaps the epistles of John (the letters to Timothy and Titus are actually manuals of ministerial instructions to two pastors who were administrators), Paul's Epistle to Philemon is a masterpiece of exquisite Christian persuasion. In it Paul marshaled his arguments simply, clearly, and beautifully, and allowed the grace of the Spirit to pervade each word and every sentence. On reading it Philemon must have been left without a single reason for not fitting in with Paul's appeals and for loving Paul and Onesimus all the more. Paul's letter to Philemon bears an even more important message to us today, and Onesimus plays the major role in conveying this. Conversion to Christianity does not release a convert from those legitimate obligations which he has contracted prior to his acceptance of Jesus as Saviour and Lord.

As a slave, Onesimus was duty bound to turn himself in to his master, not only by Roman law, but also by the far greater demands of Christian principle. As a disciple of Jesus, Onesimus was required to confess his theft to the one he had injured and to work toward restoring the money which he had purloined. Consequences notwithstanding, Onesimus as a faithful disciple must fully carry out his responsibilities. The religion of Jesus Christ does not wipe the slate clean of guilt until heartfelt repentance has brought about genuine reformation which has produced complete restitution.

Onesimus's return provided his master with the opportunity to exercise the privilege of genuine Christian forgiveness. Philemon was reminded by the Spirit through Paul's letter that he himself had been a slave to sin, but that the gospel had enabled him to exchange his lot for another Master whose will now dominated his life. The condition upon which Christ would forgive him and forget his previous conduct was his readiness to forgive and forget the past misdemeanors of Onesimus. Matthew 6:14, 15. True forgiveness is reciprocal, acting both on the one who forgives as well as on the one who is forgiven. Philemon discovered that his feelings of resentment and revenge and the thought of taking advantage of one who was cast down by guilt had no place in the heart of a subject of the kingdom of God and must be renounced immediately.

And so we leave the slave Onesimus as he walked off the page of sacred history when he walked into the home of his master Philemon. He was now a new creation and an instrument in the hand of Christ to minister in an entirely new manner to his master whom he had previously injured. In this way the runaway slave became a brother beloved and a servant of Jesus Christ, and an example to us all of what true discipleship entails in repentance and restitution to man and committal and service to God.

Ruth—Helpful Daughter-in-law

Some scholars suggest that the name Ruth may mean "Rose," and long ago someone observed that the "book of Ruth nestles like a rose between the ermine of Judges and the purple of Kings." First Samuel used to be known as First Kings. (See heading of the book title in any KJV Bible). The position of this story of Ruth in the Old Testament is remarkable. The events of the Judges end on a most sordid note. Conditions were characterized by murder, brutality, and hostility. The wail of its author is, "Every man did that which was right in his own eyes," for there was no king, not even in heaven, to discipline their lives. See Judges 17:6; 18:1; 19:1; 21:25. Spanning three centuries, the record is that of apostasy following faithfulness, ending in servitude, which eventually produced repentance and a return to God, which in turn degenerated into apostasy. And then the whole sorry process was repeated. The Lord raised up charismatic leaders who periodically roused the people to worship Him and stemmed the tide of sin for a time. This repeated sequence of delinquency and reformation makes up the context of the book of Judges during which time the story of Ruth took place.

After being disgusted by the story of wickedness in Judges and then to read the book of Ruth immediately after, is like passing from a fetid stable into the fresh air of a spring garden. That there were women like Ruth and Naomi in Israel during the time of the judges and that they should meet a man like Boaz give evidence that God has His firmament of holy ones in every age. In spite of the darkness there are stars always shining. Although there was "no king" ruling in the hearts of most Israelites, God was still upon His throne.

Ruth lived in Moab and might have died a typical Moabite woman had she not met a man. Into her hometown four Hebrew refugees from a Palestinian famine came to live. Elimelech, the name of the husband and father, means "God is my king," but he, too, did that which was right in his own eyes. He left Bethlehem, "the house of bread," because there was a famine, and came to Moab, the land of curses. See Deuteronomy 23:3-6. In his family were two good-looking young lads. Ruth soon became friendly with one of them called Mahlon, and her friendship matured into a marriage forbidden by God in Deuteronomy 7:3. Also see Ezra 9:2; and Nehemiah 13:23-25. This pagan Moabitess is thus brought into contact with the covenant people of God. But nothing seemed to work out right, for three untimely deaths followed one another. Jewish commentators suggest these were the results of divine judgment against these mixed marriages. Ruth helped to bury her father-in-law Elimelech, her husband Mahlon, and her brother-in-law Chilion, and three bereft widows were left to bemoan their lot. Elimelech had turned his back on his God-given inheritance because of the Lord's chastening famine and belied his name. Now the remnants of his family struggled for survival and identity.

It was Ruth's mother-in-law, Naomi, alone in an alien land and longing for the old place, who decided to go back home and broke the pall of sorrow and silence which blanketed the three women. She heard in Moab, the land of curses, that God had "visited his people" and supplied bread for Israel. Ruth 1:6. How she heard the rumor in a far land we are not told. God has His own ways of communicating the gospel. One day she announced that she had decided to return to her own people and suggested that her two daughters-in-law go back to their homes and try to find "rest" (fulfillment) by making the best possible efforts to patch life together again. Naomi recognized that Ruth and Orpah had treated her sons well. Ruth 1:7, 8. But she had to go. The message of hope produced action in Naomi. And as the time for parting approached, the three widow women wept. Orpah was persuaded to go back, but Ruth clung to her mother-in-law. Ruth 1:14.

One hears a great deal about mothers-in-law. They are often the butt of some wry jokes. Ruth's attitude toward hers was one of deep and abiding affection and respect. Orpah kissed Naomi and walked away sobbing. Naomi then said to Ruth, who was clinging to her, sobbing, "Behold, thy sister in law is gone back unto her people, and unto her gods: return thou after thy sister in law." Ruth 1:15. Apparently there had been some talk in the families about the claims of the true God versus the Moabite gods. The lives of the older couple had evidently tended toward influencing their neighbors for good. But now Orpah was reverting to her people and their superstitions and returning to the land of curses, and Naomi's remarks sadly point to this fact.

It was at this juncture that Ruth's true character sprang into flower. Her love for Naomi and Naomi's God blossomed. Her words sing to us across the centuries. Their poetry and pathos still move us as we listen to their cadences, and their faith and committal urge us to emulation.

> Intreat me not to leave thee,
> Or to return from following after thee:
> For whither thou goest, I will go;
> And where thou lodgest, I will lodge:
> Thy people shall be my people,

And thy God my God:
Where thou diest, will I die,
And there will I be buried:
The Lord do so to me, and more also,
If ought but death part thee and me.
    Ruth 1:16, 17.

Let us analyze what Ruth said in these lines: Do not offer me options, I will follow you. Do not try to persuade me to stay in the valley of curse. I , too, want to go where God has visited His people. There I, too, will live and rest. I leave my people of the curse for your people of blessing. I surrender my gods of lust for your God of love. The death of saints will be mine too, and I will be buried under the watching eye of God. And not even death must part us.

Ruth's phrases reveal a deep affection for the older woman, which was obviously based on genuine love and not merely loyalty to family relationship. They exhibit her acceptance of the God of the Hebrews as her own God. She had observed demonstrated in the family of the visitors from Palestine a life-style which she appreciated and which she resolved to make her own. She then affirmed that her affection would not be severed even by death. Ruth was a poet, as well as a worshiper of the true God. She was also a philosopher who had weighed alternative courses of action and then based her future plans on what she considered the best options. She was prepared to sever herself from family and kindred, race and country, and journey with her mother-in-law into a distant and unknown land, with little prospect for the future, but with a love for Naomi and trust in Naomi's God burning in her heart. Candor and action, faith and an acquisitive mind, combined to make her dramatic decision which glows across the millennia. And eventually Naomi, forlorn and desolate old Hebrew widow, and Ruth, a kind and trusting young widowed Moabite, reached Judea. From the cursed Moabite swamp Ruth, the rose, blossomed in the warmth of the love of God and rested on His heart and chosen land.

The inspired author presents Ruth, when they arrived in Bethlehem, as a thoughtful and helpful worker. She figured out a way through their difficulties. Neither of the women apparently had any funds. "Let me now go to the field and glean," she suggested. Ruth 2:2. The barley harvest, the "first fruits," was in progress, and so she volunteered to gather what she could in the fields which were closest to where they were living. Cf. Leviticus 19:9; 23:22; Deuteronomy 24:19, 21. Rather than be a burden to her mother-in-law, Ruth was not above collecting what stalks of grain she could find to help to feed the two of them.

"Her hap [luck or chance] was to light on a part of the field belonging unto Boaz." Ruth 2:3. Through the leading of God she "happened" to work in the fields of Boaz, who turned out to be a close relative of Elimelech. God always has His means prepared. As she was gleaning, she attracted the attention of the "mighty man" of wealth, the landowner. To answer his query, "Whose damsel is this?" (Ruth 2:5) we must go back to the sad story of Lot, and then add the overwhelming and transforming grace of the gospel of Christ. At Boaz's kind advice that she should rest in the field shelter and drink from the common waterpot, Ruth "fell on her face, and bowed herself to the ground, and said unto him, Why have I found grace in thine eyes, that thou shouldest take knowledge of me, seeing I am a stranger?" Ruth 2:8-10. Ruth's nature never took anything for granted. Boaz recommended that Ruth glean only in a restricted field, where he left "handfulls of purpose" to ease her task. Realizing that she was a foreigner, she knew she had no legal claim on the kindness of the landowner and was eager to express her gratitude for his kindness. Selfless, hardworking, appreciative, Ruth busied herself in trying to eke out a livelihood for Naomi and herself.

Following Boaz's gallant response, Ruth simply asked for permission to continue her gleaning. "Let me find favour in thy sight, my lord; for that thou hast comforted me, and for that thou hast spoken friendly unto thine handmaid, though I be not like unto one of thine handmaidens." Ruth 2:13. At the command of Boaz, Ruth was guarded from harm and was helped in her gleaning.

Now free to gather in his field, Ruth worked hard, and by the end of the day had a bundle of barley, which she "beat out" and took home to Naomi. Naomi was surprised at the amount she had obtained, and when she was told the whole story, realized that God was taking a hand in directing them both toward solutions of their predicaments. Boaz was actually Naomi's near "kinsman-redeemer." See Deuteronomy 25:5-10; Leviticus 25:25, 47-49.

As Naomi thought over the strange coincidence that Ruth should meet Boaz, old memories revived. She remembered her husband, and their inheritance and the laws of God governing lost patrimonies. And Naomi resolved to try to obtain the help of Boaz in regaining their forfeited heritage. Her plan appears to us today as a strange one. Calling Ruth to her, she explained what she had decided. Ruth was to go quietly into the area in which Boaz slept and curl up at his feet, as was often the custom of servants. When he awakened she was to explain the circumstances to him of the lost inheritance of Naomi and her scheme to regain it, and then act on whatever he proposed. Ruth 3:2-5. Naomi now had come to trust that God was working out His grand design for them both.

At midnight Boaz awakened with a start to discover a woman at his feet, and "was afraid." Ruth 3:8. His character and reputation were at stake, and he did not wish to compromise them. Ruth's response deserves close study. "I am Ruth thine handmaid," she said candidly, and then asked, "spread therefore thy skirt

over thine handmaid; for thou art a near kinsman."
Ruth 3:9. Her word for kinsman was the Hebrew *goel*.
It described a relative who makes sacrifices for the redemption of his own people, and is typical of Jesus, the
Kinsman-Redeemer of our race. Ruth reminded the
conscientious Boaz of his responsibility as Naomi's
goel, suggesting he should do what the law required for
the lost heritage of Elimelech. Her request for Boaz's
"skirt" to be spread over her was an invitation to him
to marry her. See Ezekiel 16:8.

The law of redemption applied not only to property, but also to the restoration of family lineage. Deuteronomy 25:7-10. Elimelech and his sons had died and
left no heir. The kinsman-redeemer was therefore
duty bound to try to build the family line of Elimelech
by marrying the woman who could produce an heir
who should inherit Elimelech's property and family title and guarantee the continuation of his name. As the
implication of what Ruth had said to him sunk into his
mind, Boaz was ready to act. He explained to her that
while he was indeed a near kinsman, there was one
who was even closer than he. He promised that on the
morrow he would set in motion the legal processes by
which the heritage might be restored to Ruth. If the
true *goel* was unable to play his part, Boaz promised
that he would step in to do whatever should be done.

Early the next morning the town council was called,
and Boaz explained the problem to the city fathers, and
to the *goel* or next of kin of Elimelech. Boaz then offered his relative the privilege of performing the rites of
the *goel*. Ruth 4:1-4. This man was ready to purchase
the field and restore it to Naomi. But then Boaz reminded him that there was a further duty to be carried
out. He must marry Ruth, and their child would be
Elimelech's heir. The *goel* refused to do this, as his
own name might be extinguished in Israel. And so the
privilege of the *goel* was assumed by Boaz. The
property was purchased and restored, and soon there

54

was a marriage between Ruth and Boaz. The boy that was born to this union was called Obed, who became the grandfather of David. And it is for this reason that Ruth the Moabitess is recorded in the genealogy of Jesus of Nazareth, the Son of man. Matthew 1:5. Her name stands alongside that of Boaz, who by his righteous behavior obtained an immortal name in the roster of God's people.

When Ruth set out from Kerak in Moab for unknown Bethlehem in Judea, she had no idea what the Lord had in store for her. She simply felt that she must do the right thing and be kind to her mother-in-law. She was also resolved to be faithful to the true God whom she now worshiped and who, she evidently felt, could not be served should she remain among her kindred. And the Lord whom she adored had a future for her which she could never have imagined. I wonder whether she had been tempted to return to her folk and the young men she knew. I wonder whether love and loyalty toward Naomi debated with youth and pleasure for a season. I wonder whether she later caught her breath in fear as she realized how close she had come to missing her destiny. But thank God, she made the right decision and stuck to it. God honored her choice and gave her a reward above anything she might have asked or thought.

God honors all who honor Him. He was looking for the very qualities which Ruth possessed to embed in the lineage from which His Son should come. It mattered not to Him that she was a foreigner, a Moabite, from a cursed tribe which was about to be exterminated because of persistent wickedness. Origins matter little to God, and birth is of no consequence. Man originated from dust! What is of eternal consequence is the new birth, and then what is done with the new God-given life, which His child is free to use for His glory. Penniless, outcast, pagan, widowed, cursed, and thus shown to be unworthy in the eyes of her peers, Ruth was chosen by God for a role almost as important as that later fulfilled by the maid of Nazareth. David came from Ruth, and the poetry of her soul found fruition in the psalms which her great-grandson penned.

When she turned her back on Moab and Moab's gods and left her all and went out into the unknown with God and Naomi, Ruth started along a path which was to lead down the centuries to the manger and the heritage she shared with her greatest Son, the Kinsman-Redeemer of the world. And in the golden mists of the future, somewhere near the glory of the throne of the Greater than her son David, Ruth, the transformed Moabitess, will sit watching happily, grateful for the part which Providence had for her in the unfolding sweep of the story of redemption.

Barnabas—Supportive Friend

If it hadn't been for Barnabas, I wonder what would have happened to Saul. Barnabas is one of the most underrated leaders of the early church. Born in Cyprus and given the name of Joseph, worked to Joses on the tongue of the Greeks, he was a Levite who possessed a piece of property. These facts are recorded in the inspired introduction to his life. Acts 4:36, 37. How he came to become a Christian and what he was doing in Jerusalem we are not told. Perhaps he was fulfilling his Levitical duties in the temple. But in this opening passage concerning him a very wonderful attitude is noted. He was the first among the early Christians who exercised sacrificial generosity toward the needy members of the church. He saw that many believers in Jerusalem had been rendered homeless and hungry because of the severity of the Jewish persecution against the Christians, and he remembered that he was only a steward of the means entrusted to him by the Lord. He studied his resources and decided to sell his land and donate the money realized to the apostles, to be used by them as they saw fit.

Barnabas is the first Christian philanthropist. His example of generosity might have influenced Ananias and Sapphira to pledge their property and to dispose of it to the same end. But they later held back part of the profit which they had realized and pretended that their donation was the whole amount. The stories of Barnabas and Ananias and Sapphira are placed side by side so that the contrast might be seen and studied. It was probably because of the help and comfort which the munificence of Joseph provided to the destitute Christians that induced the apostles to name him Barnabas, "son of consolation," or "comfort," or "encouragement." It is in this setting that his new name appears. This Aramaic name (*Bar Nabi*) may mean "son of prophecy," with all that the words *prophecy* and *prophet* suggest of the representative and spokesmen of God. The Greek translation of his name *parakleseōs*, takes our minds back to the same word which our Lord used to designate the Holy Spirit (*parakletos*, translated Comforter), whom He was about to send to take His place. John 14:16. It literally means one who is called to one's side in a time of need for assurance and help.

Some three or four years after these events, the Scriptures record that Barnabas was still in the church at Jerusalem and still had not been elected to a position of importance. Meanwhile Saul of Tarsus had become the most notorious persecutor of Christians and had been on the rampage since the stoning of Stephen. The believers in the city were terrified and suffering dire trials. To cap it all, the church was further shaken by the unbelievable news that Saul had passed through some kind of crisis on his way to Damascus and now claimed to be a Christian! I can imagine how the rumors flew concerning what had happened, most of them, of course, fantastic and untrue! And then to the consternation of every disciple, Saul of Tarsus arrived back in Jerusalem and tried to infiltrate the ranks of the believers. Some suspected that he was a trickster, or worse; while others, overly cautious, gave him the cold shoulder and maintained a watch-and-see attitude. Acts 9:26.

At this crisis the character of Barnabas was revealed. His shrewd knowledge of human nature and his talent of discernment enabled him to size up the new Saul of Tarsus and conclude that he was now a completely transformed and trustworthy man. He had faith in Saul's genuine conversion. This was established on his personal contact and investigation. After this he "took him, and brought him to the apostles, and declared unto them how he had seen the Lord in the way, and that he had spoken to him, and how he had preached boldly at Damascus in the name of Jesus. And he was with them coming in and going out of Jerusalem. And he spake boldly in the name of the Lord Jesus, and disputed against the Grecians: but they went about to slay him." Acts 9:27-29.

Consider the interesting contributions which three outstanding men made to the conversion of Saul of Tarsus and his progress toward the kingdom of Christ. The dying Stephen witnessed to him and then prayed for the forgiveness of his sins; the fearful Ananias instructed him in the gospel and then baptized him; and the kindly Barnabas personally investigated the factors of his conversion and then vouched for him to the church. And in this way Saul's career was launched. Barnabas took Paul before the apostles in Jerusalem and declared how Paul had met the Lord on the road to Damascus and how his life had been dramatically changed. Barnabas had had enough of this indecision and shilly-shallying on the part of the believers and decided to precipitate a crisis of decision. I can see him encouraging everybody, not only Saul, but also the apostles and other Christian leaders to do the right thing. And thus a friendship was established between Barnabas the Levite and Saul the Pharisee which lasted, in spite of some traumatic episodes, until the end of their lives.

Following the martyrdom of Stephen, the Jewish Sanhedrin, led by Saul, violently persecuted the church. This induced many of the believers to flee the capital and take up residence in distant towns. In this way the divine purposes were fulfilled and Christianity was planted in other communities. Acts 11:19-21. Antioch was one of the more important of these centers, where a goodly company of believers was established. Sensing the need for further aggressive evangelistic work in this city, the apostles at Jerusalem sent Barnabas to preach the gospel in that area. "Who, when he came, and had seen the grace of God, was glad, and exhorted them all, that with purpose of heart they would cleave unto the Lord." Acts 11:23. Here again we encounter a pun based on his nickname! Barnabas "exhorted" or "comforted" them (*parekalei*). He was still the one whom people loved to call to their sides for aid! And as he told the story Luke felt compelled to launch into a description of the sort of person Barnabas really was. The church historian recorded by Inspiration that "he was a good man, and full of the Holy Ghost and of faith: and much people was added unto the Lord." Acts 11:24. What a loving and sincere Spirit-filled pastor Barnabas was, and this gave him great evangelistic success! Barnabas was not a famous theologian as was Paul, nor was he an orator. But God used the talents he dedicated to His service, and good success in his mission resulted. Even the heathen thought of Barnabas as the father figure in their divine pantheon. Acts 14:12.

Realizing from the large harvest of souls which had been garnered into the Lord's church that there were many others to be harvested, Barnabas, because he was practical and farseeing, immediately sensed that he needed help to shepherd the lambs and sheep. And he also knew instinctively the man who would give the best help. He had last heard that he was living in Tarsus. And because Barnabas still had faith and confidence in him, he personally set out for "Tarsus, for to seek Saul: and when he had found him, he brought him unto Antioch. And it came to pass, that a whole year they assembled themselves with the church, and taught much people." Acts 11:25, 26. Barnabas had grasped the need clearly, and knew exactly what to do to meet it.

Antioch in Syria was a Gentile city, and most of the converts to Christianity had come from heathenism. Barnabas remembered that in his initial commission to Saul of Tarsus, Ananias had informed him that Christ thought of him as "a chosen vessel unto me, to bear my name before the Gentiles." Acts 9:15. How free from carping Jewish prejudice Barnabas was! Instead of ignoring or discouraging the Gentile church at Antioch, he obtained for them the best pastor he could find, one who had been commissioned by Heaven for this very special ministry. The two apostles were so effective in their proclamation of Christ and His gospel that a nickname was invented for the disciples. They were first called Christians in Antioch. Acts. 11:26. Barnabas never ceased his encouragement and help to every person whom he touched, and it was he who put Saul to work for Christ and stayed with him until he was trained.

For perhaps half a dozen years Barnabas and Saul worked closely together, and the church at Antioch grew strong under their joint ministry. It was at Antioch that they were both ordained and sent out by the church as the first Christian foreign missionaries. Acts 13:1-3. As their companion, they took with them the nephew of Barnabas (Colossians 4:10), John Mark by name (Acts 13:5; also see Acts 15:37, 38). But after only a few months of travel, the young man, terrified by the harsh reception given to the missionaries by the pagans among whom they worked, and perhaps overcome by homesickness, decided to quit and return home (Acts 13:13), while he left Paul and Barnabas to continue their itinerating evangelism undaunted. It was because of this event that the leadership of the party shifted. Henceforth, Luke noted, it was "Paul and

Barnabas" who did this or that, or went hither and thither.

On their return to their home base at the end of their tour, Paul and Barnabas found themselves at the vortex of vigorous theological discussion, and even hostile conflict. Acts 15:1-5. The story was being bruited about that they were forsaking Judaism and breaking the ancient Hebrew laws. The truth of the matter was that while the Gentiles were joyous at becoming Christians, neither they nor Paul and Barnabas thought that they should also become Jews! The two leaders then played their parts in the church convention called by the apostles in resolving the racial, social, and theological problems this attitude had bred.

Sometime following the first council of the Christian church held at Jerusalem to settle this issue (Acts 15:6-23), Paul and Barnabas decided that it was time to set out on a second missionary journey (Acts 15:36-39). The gentle, tolerant and comforting Barnabas wanted to give John Mark a second chance and take him along again, but Paul would have none of this. Mark had failed them in a crisis and consequently was not to be trusted. So warm did the discussion grow that both Barnabas and Paul thoroughly disagreed (Acts 15:39), according to Luke's term! As the result the two missionaries decided that they had reached the parting of the ways. Barnabas then took Mark and went off to evangelize his home island of Cyprus, while Paul chose Silas as his companion and traveled through familiar Tarsus in Cilicia. Each leader chose his home base from which to launch out on their efforts to spread the gospel. Barnabas was still the encourager, and how his encouragement of Mark paid off was noted by none other than Paul himself years later! Mark "is profitable to me for the ministry" (2 Timothy 4:11), he wrote to Timothy at the end of his life.

But in spite of his many virtues Barnabas was not without faults. Paul remembered that at one point during a visit of some of the Jewish Christian leaders from Jerusalem to Antioch, Peter refused to eat with Gentile Christians, although he had done this before the Judaising brethren arrived in the city. As he told the story later, Paul added the telling insight, "Barnabas also was carried away with their dissimulation." Galatians 2:13. Even good men may make mistakes. But thank God Barnabas listened to the sharp rebuke of his friend and matured in his faithful service to his Lord.

Luke remembered the moving description which James had given concerning the returned missionaries. On their arrival at Jerusalem to represent the Gentile churches, the leader of the Jewish Christian community had observed, "Our beloved Barnabas and Paul, men that have hazarded their lives for the name of our Lord Jesus Christ" (Acts 15:25, 26) are now present! With Paul, Barnabas had placed himself on the altar of sacrifice and often risked his life for his Lord. Twice during his lifetime Barnabas had staked his reputation and his future on what he considered to be the right decision! He had vouched for Saul and had kept faith with John Mark. Comfort, when it was needed most, was what Barnabas had most to give. Support when men were left alone in suspicion or criticism was what Barnabas supplied richly. He was ready to respond when called to the side of those who needed a friend in deed.

Inspiration remembers Barnabas as the human *paraklete* and the spiritual pastor, a man of faith and good philanthropic works, a church promoter and an ardent missionary, and a molder of men. All this is encompassed by the perceptive inspired description, "He was a good man."

Abigail—Understanding Wife

We would never have got to know Abigail if her husband had not been a drunken fool at the time David was being hunted by Saul like a partridge on the heath. At that time David's only aim in life was to stay ahead of Saul's hit men, and this drove him to the mountainous country of Carmel and the wilderness of Paran in Judea. In the vicinity a wealthy landowner by the name of Nabal lived in luxury with his wise and beautiful wife Abigail. 1 Samuel 25:2, 3. It was the season of sheep shearing, and David, realizing that this was a time when Nabal counted his profits and that his wealth was rapidly increasing, asked for assistance. His messengers pointed out to Nabal that they and their companions had protected his family and his flocks from all marauders. Nabal's servants readily acknowledged the truth of this claim and the great service David's men had rendered. 1 Samuel 25:15, 16.

Nabal, however, churlish and evil at best (1 Samuel 25:3), rebuffed David's messengers by reminding them that David had defected from Saul and that he, Nabal, would not waste his resources on persons of whose origins and status he was ignorant (1 Samuel 25:10, 11). When David received this rude and unnecessary rebuke, he was furious and immediately marshaled his forces, determined to exterminate Nabal and his family and destroy everything he possessed. It is at this juncture that Abigail comes into the story.

The historian continues, "But one of the young men told Abigail, Nabal's wife, saying, Behold, David sent messengers out of the wilderness to salute our master; and he railed on them. But the men were very good unto us, and we were not hurt, neither missed we any thing, as long as we were conversant with them, when we were in the fields: they were a wall unto us both by night and day, all the while we were with them keeping the sheep. Now therefore know and consider what thou wilt do; for evil is determined against our master, and against all his household: for he is such a son of Belial, that a man cannot speak to him." 1 Samuel 25:14-17.

Hearing this report Abigail knew exactly what to do and when to do it. She did not talk it over with her husband, because she was well aware of what he would say. So she packed abundant supplies of the necessities of life for David and his men and sent them ahead on mules in the charge of her servants. Then she herself set out to plead with David. The two parties soon came face-to-face. Abigail immediately dismounted and bowed herself in obeisance before David. In contrast with Nabal's curt, "Who is David?" Abigail addressed him as "My Lord." Taking full responsibility for Nabal's behavior, she requested an opportunity quietly to talk the matter over with David. "With kind words she sought to soothe his irritated feelings, and she pleaded with him in behalf of her husband. With nothing of ostentation or pride, but full of the wisdom and love of God, Abigail revealed the strength of her devotion to her household; and she made it plain to David that the unkind course of her husband was in no wise premeditated against him as a personal affront, but was simply the outburst of an unhappy and selfish nature."—*Patriarchs and Prophets*, p. 666.

Abigail begged David not to seek needless vengeance and reminded him that it was actually God who was now holding him back from committing an act of rash and needless murder. "Abigail did not take to herself the credit of this reasoning to turn David from his hasty purpose, but gave to God the honor and the praise. She then offered her rich provision as a peace offering to the men of David, and still pleaded as if she herself were the one who had so excited the resentment of the chief."—*Ibid.*

As she continued to reason with him, "Abigail presented by implication the course that David ought to pursue. He should fight the battles of the Lord. He was not to seek revenge for personal wrongs, even though persecuted as a traitor."—*Ibid.* She continued with sentences that are almost prophetic! "The soul of my lord shall be bound in the bundle of life with the Lord thy God. . . . And it shall come to pass, when the Lord shall have done to my lord according to all the good that he hath spoken concerning thee, and shall have appointed thee prince over Israel; that this shall be no grief unto thee, nor offense of heart unto my lord, either that thou hast shed blood causeless, or that my lord hath avenged himself: and when the Lord shall have dealt well with my lord, then remember thine handmaid." 1 Samuel 25:29-31, RV.

"These words could have come only from the lips of one who had partaken of the wisdom from above. The piety of Abigail, like the fragrance of a flower, breathed out all unconsciously in face and word and action. The Spirit of the Son of God was abiding in her soul. Her speech, seasoned with grace, and full of kindness and peace, shed a heavenly influence. Better inpulses came to David, and he trembled as he thought what might have been the consequences of his rash purpose."—*Ibid.*, p. 667.

"Abigail was a wise reprover and counselor. David's passion died away under the power of her influence and reasoning. He was convinced that he had taken an unwise course and had lost control of his own spirit."—*Ibid.*

On her return home Abigail was surprised and shocked to find her husband and his cronies in the midst of a drunken revelry all unmindful of the tragedy which might have resulted from his foolish words. And so she waited until he had sobered up the next morning before she told him of her adventures and how close he had come to an untimely and violent death. So shocked was Nabal, "a coward at heart when he realized how near his folly had brought him to a sudden death, [that] he seemed smitten with paralysis. Fearful that David would still pursue his purpose of revenge, he was filled with horror, and sank down in a condition of helpless insensibility. After ten days he died."—*Ibid.*, p. 668.

If ever a person's character is revealed by the words spoken, Abigail's speech exhibits the kind of thinking that made up her life. She was perfectly frank and made no attempt to cover up the insults which had been flung at David by her husband or to make any excuses for them. She herself took the blame for it all and confessed, "I thine handmaid saw not the young men of my lord, whom thou didst send." 1 Samuel 25:25. The implication is that had she known of David's request there would have been a different kind of response. Then she begged pardon for her fault, because she had been unaware of the circumstances, "I pray thee, forgive the trespass of thine handmaid," she pleaded. 1 Samuel 25:28.

Abigail had a profound knowledge of human nature and the consequences of human conduct. She reminded David that in later and more calm moments he would remember the rash deed of revenge he was planning and would deeply regret it. She implored him not to act in such a way that he would afterward realize with grief that he had offended God. 1 Samuel 25:31. What a telling argument! And David immediately sensed its truthfulness. His response is a moving tri-

67

bute to his good sense, humility, and righteousness. "Praise be to the Lord, the God of Israel, who has sent you today to meet me. May you be blessed for your good judgment and for keeping me from bloodshed this day and from avenging myself with my own hands. Otherwise, as surely as the Lord, the God of Israel, lives, who has kept me from harming you, if you had not come quickly to meet me, not one male belonging to Nabal would have been left alive by daybreak." 1 Samuel 25:32-34, NIV.

Abigail knew how to handle people because she had learned to handle herself. How long after her marriage she discovered the sort of man with whom she was linked I do not know, but she must have learned soon enough that he was stupid, churlish, cowardly, mean, and cantankerous. She candidly reminded David that she was well aware of the fact that he lived in the manner suggested by his name, Nabal, meaning stupid. Then she said in effect, Don't take any notice of him! She had evidently developed this attitude herself. She was stuck with him, and there was little she could do about it. So she had decided to do the best she was able in the circumstances, avoiding open confrontations, humoring him whenever she could, and in this way had managed his and her affairs very well. She had also developed a close understanding with her servants, who did not hesitate to talk frankly with Abigail about their master's folly. One of them even observed, "He is such a son of Belial, that a man cannot speak to him." 1 Samuel 25:17. All this shows Abigail to be a very open and perceptive, understanding and cooperative person. She was in control of her feelings at all times and did not go about repining her lot.

Abigail was also a woman of deep religious convictions. Her speech to David is full of allusions to the workings of Providence. She claimed that God was the One who had restrained David's avenging sword, and affirmed that He would one day fulfill the promise made at David's annointing and place him upon the throne of Israel. 1 Samuel 25:26, 30. She was confident that David would survive Saul and his assassins and assured him that his life was "bound in the bundle of life with the Lord thy God." 1 Samuel 25:29. What a lovely way of telling David that his times were in God's hands and that underneath were the everlasting arms! Because she was certain that the Lord would carry out all His promises and predictions concerning David, her final appeal requested, "When the Lord shall have dealt well with my lord, then remember thine handmaid." 1 Samuel 25:31.

And David certainly did! He was so impressed with her that after the death of her husband "he sent and communed with Abigail, to take her to him to wife." 1 Samuel 25:39. And to his proposal of marriage she responded with touching humility, "Behold, let thine handmaid be a servant to wash the feet of the servants of my lord." 1 Samuel 25:41. In all her speeches—and she says more in the brief space allotted her in the Bible than most characters—she reveals a disposition totally void of selfishness. There does not ever obtrude a desire to appear center stage. Because of her modesty, her knowledge of human nature, her understanding of her own place in life, she shows herself at all times the wise and gentle peacemaker.

She made no attempt to take her life in her own hands and escape from a hard situation with her boorish husband. She learned to get along with him and his ways and to maintain a right relationship with her fellows and her God. In His own good time and way the Lord allowed circumstances to develop so that she unexpectedly had her burden removed and found herself free to live her life. The Lord allowed the very person who had ignorantly been bent on her destruction to become her husband. By trusting and waiting, while making the best of conditions she could not alter, Abigail allowed God to work out His design for her life.

And by his marriage to Nabal's widow David would gain the rich estate which was now Abigail's. The Lord shows Himself the Master of the affairs of those who submit to His rule.

The last words of Abigail recorded in Scripture (1 Sam. 25:41) echo the sentiments of the Servant of servants as He bowed low to wash the feet of the servants of the Divine Master. And as we watch Abigail borne upon the shoulders of her servants to be married to David, we wistfully imagine the bride of Christ borne on angels' wings to the marriage of the Greater than David. Abigail's road to victory was paved with willing, humble service, and the Lord in His good time and way changed her "old husband" the fool for her "new husband" David, the progenitor of the Messiah.

Eliezer—Devoted Steward

An unnamed family of Syrians from Damascus joined their fortunes with Abraham as he traveled south. A son was born to this family in the patriarch's vast encampment. They named him Eliezer, "God is my helper." Genesis 15:2, 3. The character and abilities of the lad caught the eye of Abraham, and through the years Eliezer came to be regarded as a member of the family. When they concluded that they could not have a child of their own Abraham and Sarah considered adopting Eliezer, a devoted servant they had come to love and trust, as their son and heir.

Abraham had been in Palestine for some twenty years when Eliezer is introduced to us at a moving crisis in the unfolding drama of the covenant story. Long before this, the patriarch had answered the divine summons to leave his city Ur and his homeland Chaldea and say good-bye to his kindred. He and his wife Sarah had set out on an uncharted pilgrimage, which was to take them to strange lands and into stranger adventures. Through the years they had maintained their trust in God. Their faith had strengthened, and Abraham was learning to obey the Lord's slightest requirement implicitly.

On occasion the Lord had reiterated His promise to the patriarch that his posterity should inherit the land of Canaan. But decade after decade Abraham and his wife remained childless. After the third time the promise was made, imagining that it was now impossible for them to have a child, Abraham pleaded with the Lord that his trusty servant Eliezer should be adopted as son and then accepted as the surrogate heir. Genesis 15:2. See *Patriarchs and Prophets*, p. 136. Although this request at first appears innocent and even helpful, it was actually a demonstration of a lack of faith in God's pledged word and an insult to the power of the Lord to carry out His design. But God assured His naïve follower that his own son should soon be the inheritor. And then the Heavenly Visitor, without rebuking him, kindly and gently led Abraham out into the night and showed him the stars, promising that his descendants should be more numerous. And this time Abraham again affirmed that he "believed in the Lord" (Genesis 15:6), but his faith was still partial (Genesis 16:1-4).

In the years which followed, Eliezer continued to serve his master faithfully. He quietly observed Abraham marry Sarah's maid, Hagar, and have a son whom he called Ishmael. This lad was regarded by the patriarch and his family as the heir and loaded with all the benefits and privileges of his position. We notice that during a vision thirteen years later, Abraham pleaded with God, "O that Ishmael might live before thee," meaning, be accepted as my heir. Genesis 17:18. But God reiterated His promise that he and Sarah should have a son of their own. Genesis 17:19.

After this brief mention of Eliezer we hear nothing more of him for almost half a century. During those hidden years in Canaan he remained faithful to his master, who came to rely upon him implicitly, and who loved him intensely. Abraham considered Eliezer as "his eldest servant" and set him up as the master "over all that he had" (Genesis 24:2) as well as making him the steward of his house (Genesis 15:2). At the conclusion of the half century since we first read of Eliezer we are informed that "all the goods of his master'' were entrusted to his care. Genesis 24:10.

In the meantime Isaac, the promised heir, had been born, and Eliezer watched solicitously as he grew to manhood. Hagar and Ishmael had rebelled against God's choice of the heir and had been expelled.

When the young man Isaac was forty years old Abraham felt it was time he married. The patriarch resolved that Isaac should not make Ishmael's mistake and marry a Canaanite woman. To help him he called his trusted friend Eliezer and entered into a covenant with him to find a suitable wife! Eliezer was to look for her among Abraham's kin. Isaac should on no account return to Mesopotamia to fetch her home. Should the woman prove unwilling to come to Canaan, Eliezer should consider himself discharged from the conditions of the contract and return alone. See Genesis 24:1-9.

The story of Eliezer's quest for Isaac's bride is a detailed chronicle of providential leading and answered prayers. It portrays the wisdom and faith of Eliezer and teaches us how God and man can cooperate to achieve success.

Eliezer immediately loaded ten camels with sufficient provisions for the journey, as well as with gifts for the bride. He then set out on his long trek to Haran, ''the city of Nahor,'' where some of the relatives of Abraham were known to live. Genesis 24:10. While on this journey of some six hundred miles, Eliezer carefully pondered his strategy. Reaching his destination in the late afternoon, he went to the watering hole to await the women. He figured that since Isaac lived a pastoral life, his wife should understand the needs of the encampment and of his extensive flocks.

As he waited, Eliezer reminded the Lord that he was doing his best to fulfill the divine mandate for Abraham to have the right posterity. He realized that among all the women of Haran he could not possibly find the right one without the help of Heaven. He then proposed a sign to the Lord which he was ready to take as an indication that he was on the right track. It was this. The woman of whom he should ask a drink and who would volunteer to water his camels was the prospective bride of Isaac. He thought that one who was prepared to draw water for ten thirsty camels, as well as a group of drivers, would make a hard-working and hospitable, kind and considerate wife. Read the full account in *Patriarchs and Prophets,* p. 172, 173, and Genesis 24.

Hardly had Eliezer finished praying when the women and their flocks were there. His attention was attracted by one with "courteous manners" and who "was very fair to look upon." In his eagerness he "ran" to make his request to her. To his amazement she gave the precise response for which he had just asked in his prayer. And as she carried out her self-imposed tasks, Eliezer kept wondering whether she might indeed be the woman of destiny. Read the full story in Genesis 24:15-67.

After the men and animals had slaked their thirst, he presented her with a golden gift and inquired her name. Informed that she was the granddaughter of Nahor, Abraham's brother, Eliezer was overwhelmed with joy and gratitude. Hearing her offering him lodging for his entire party, he sensed that God was indeed leading, and right there by the well, amid all the noise and chatter, and in full sight of all the other women who were busy watering animals and filling their vessels, "the man bowed down his head, and worshipped the Lord." Meanwhile Rebekah, for that was her name, had run home to inform her family that a visitor had come all the way from the camp of Abraham.

Her brother Laban, who appears to have been the chief of the clan, immediately hurried out to meet Eliezer, curious to learn the identity of one who had presented such a rich earring and rich bracelets to his sister. His eager "Come in, thou blessed of the Lord" betrays his true feelings, which were stirred by more than generous hospitality! In the scriptural stories which follow, Laban is revealed as a totally mercenary person. Years later he used and exploited Jacob, his sister Rebekah's son, to meet his personal and family needs.

Arriving at the home of Laban and Rebekah, Eliezer was quickly made to feel at ease, while his animals and companions were being bedded down. But before he would even stop to eat or make himself comfortable, he felt that he had to discharge his commission. When the clan had assembled, he carefully outlined the story of the call of Abraham to possess the Land of Canaan and soon came to the immediate need of finding a suitable wife for Isaac, the son and heir. Eliezer explained the basis upon which the venture was to be carried out. The bride, he told the family of Nahor, must voluntarily come to Canaan, and Isaac must on no condition return to Mesopotamia. He recounted his prayers and the amazingly prompt answers which God had given. He emphasized the felicitous providence which had brought him directly to the only home in the whole country in which a suitable bride was available. He then pointed to Rebekah as the fulfillment of the divine design.

Abraham had probably prayed before Eliezer and his party had set out. Eliezer had prayed on the way and then again at the well. He had prayed silently yet again while Rebekah was watering the animals, and had publicly bowed in thanksgiving on his discovery that she belonged to the right family. He then affirmed that Abraham had assured him that he would be angelled in his way. He noted that he himself had asked the Lord to prosper his way. And he stressed that because he had started in the appointed way, the Lord had led him along "the right way." He ended his testimony on divine guidance by declaring that his way had indeed "prospered." Then he made the appeal which was the purpose of his venture: "And now if ye will deal truly and kindly with my master, tell me: and if not, tell me; that I may turn to the right hand, or to the left." Genesis 24:49. He sensed that Providence had brought him to the climax of his mission. Eliezer was certainly clear in his thinking and prompt in his acting. The moment of truth had arrived, and the decision must be made now!

Without any argument, Laban readily agreed that the Lord had obviously arranged the circumstances and replied that as far as he was concerned Rebekah had his permission to leave to become the wife of Abraham's son. And now once more, in front of all present, Eliezer fell on his knees and thanked God as he worshiped His holy name. Only then was the steward of Abraham ready to distribute the rich gifts he had brought for Rebekah and her family and to settle down for a good meal and a quiet night's rest.

Early the next morning Eliezer was impatient to be off, but his host wanted to delay his return for a while. Perhaps he thought that he might extract even more rich gifts from his guest! Thinking that Rebekah might fit in with his plan to hold off her departure, Laban suggested that she be consulted. To his question "Wilt thou go with this man?" she replied without hesitation, "I will go," and that was that! After his stay in the city of Nahor for only some fifteen hours, Eliezer was on his way back to Hebron, his mission accomplished more easily and swiftly than he had imagined.

We are told nothing of the return trip, which took weeks of joyous anticipation. Meanwhile Isaac expectantly waited to see the outcome of Eliezer's mission. Inspiration simply and movingly grants us a glimpse into his soul. As was his habit Isaac went out to pray in the field at evening. If ever a marriage was arranged on the foundation of prayer, this one was! One evening, as Isaac was praying, he became aware that a caravan

76

was coming, he hoped including his wife-to-be. As the caravan approached, Rebekah saw a man in the distance pensively walking in the gloaming. With rising excitement she inquired of Eliezer who he might be, intuitively sensing the presence of her future husband. On learning his identity she quickly dismounted and covered herself with her veil, for it was the custom that she must not be seen by him until their wedding day.

What an exciting story Eliezer had to tell Abraham and Isaac that evening. And then the Scripture narrative ends as simply as it began, "And Isaac . . . took Rebekah, and she became his wife; and he loved her." Genesis 24:67.

In this idyl, the outcome of which was the eventual birth of the Messiah and the salvation of the world, the real unsung hero is Eliezer. He had served Abraham for some sixty years, doing whatever was required of him. Trustworthy and responsible, he grew to stature in this household until everything Abraham possessed was placed in his charge. More than fifty years before, Abraham had considered adopting Eliezer as his heir. But then had come the fulfillment of the promise that Abraham's own son should be the heir.

Eliezer's story has always reminded me of the Baptist, who for some time stood center stage. Yet with the coming of his cousin Jesus, he could happily say, "He must increase, but I must decrease." John 3:30. Jesus called him "the friend of the bridegroom" (John 3:29) whose responsibility it was to act as the go-between to introduce the couple, Christ and His church, to each other and to make the necessary arrangement with the families concerned for the "marriage of the Lamb." Revelation 19:7.

Eliezer carried out every task entrusted to him with love and humility, never obtrusive, always prompt, never brash or self-assertive, always gentle and steadfast.

At the marriage of Isaac and Rebekah, Eliezer must

have been a pleased and quiet participant, kindly, smiling, helpful. He was part of the family of Abraham, and yet he was not. As the Scriptures close his story we are left feeling better because we have come to know this pious man of prayer, delighted with his relationship with Abraham and dedicated in his service to Abraham's God. He evokes in us the desire to be as trustworthy and faithful to our calling. Always satisfied with his role, he quietly slips out of the picture he had helped to frame, while the bright lights focus on Isaac and Rebekah and ultimately the Heir of promise.

Dorcas—Resurrected Worker

Dorcas, the Christian worker of Joppa, is one of the few persons in all history whom God has chosen to resurrect. She had evidently been sick for some time before her death. This may raise theological questions. Why did God allow such a good and active Christian to get sick? This problem was posed long ago by the friends of Job. His experience provides conclusive evidence that sometimes even the "perfect" (Job 2:3) may be allowed to get sick "without a cause" as a means to spread the knowledge of God and of the machinations of Satan. And even at their deaths the word from the eternal throne is "Blessed are the dead which die in the Lord." Revelation 14:13.

When Dorcas died her friends prepared her body for burial (Acts 9:37), but hope still lived. Learning that the apostle Peter was visiting the nearby church at Lydda, they remembered the words of Christ (John 11:25), and their hopes soared. They immediately sent a delegation of two to invite Peter to come to help them in their dire need. Did these believers really think that Peter's prayer or presence would raise Dorcas to life? The story strongly suggests that these young Christians did have a strong and simple faith to this end. They begged him not to delay his coming. Their faith emerges as almost incredible to us; today we might even describe it as naïve. And so Peter must wonderingly have set out upon what was to become an uncommon and remarkable adventure.

Her name in her Aramaic-speaking home was Tabitha (Acts (9:40), which was translated by her Greek friends as Dorcas. It means a fawn or gazelle in both languages. This nickname suggests that her fellow Christians sensed that her energy and alertness, her gentleness and swiftness were fitly represented in her name. The roe or female deer is the guardian of the herd. In the love song of Solomon, his beloved is likened to a doe (Song of Solomon 2:9), an endearing epithet often applied to a gentle and affectionate woman in Bible times.

When the apostle Peter reached Joppa, he went straight to the home in which the body of Dorcas lay. There he was met by a sad group of mourners, including "the widows [who] stood by him weeping, and shewing the coats and garments which Dorcas made, while she was with them." Acts 9:39. In the light of Dorcas's life of unselfish service "it is little wonder that they mourned," writes Ellen White in *The Acts of the Apostles,* page 132, "that warm teardrops fell upon the inanimate clay." Joppa, the town in which Dorcas lived, was a seaport from whose harbor many mariners sailed across the seven seas. In those days the frail, wooden craft faced terrible odds, and some of the sailors never returned. Their widows and children needed immediate help and solace, and Dorcas had generously provided both.

Peter's heart was moved with sympathy for the helpless, needy ones, and he was impressed by the Spirit to ask God for an uncommon boon. But he first of all directed that the visitors should leave the room of death. This lesson he had learned long before, when he had accompanied his Master to the death chamber of the daughter of Jairus. Luke 8:51. All the doubting and curious must be excluded from the room of special prayer. When he was alone, Peter knelt down and prayed that God would restore Dorcas to life, and then, calling her by her Aramaic name, as his master Jesus had done to the daughter of Jairus, bade her arise. Cf. Matthew 9:25; Mark 5:41. The Lord immediately honored his petition of faith and the hope and trust of the other Christians. When Dorcas opened her eyes, she saw Peter looking at her and immediately sat up, her sickness gone, her life and strength restored. The God who had raised her could as easily have helped her to stand, but He left this office to His representative to perform. Peter proffered a helping hand and then happily presented the resurrected woman in the full glow of health to her now joyful friends. Acts 9:40, 41.

What sort of a person qualifies to be resurrected by God? We meet a very few of them in the Old and New Testaments. Christ Himself raised some, while Elijah and Elisha, Paul and Peter raised others, all by the power of God. Why are most individuals left in death, while certain others are granted a second lease on life? In the case of Dorcas, we are given some pointers to answer our questions. Let us seek to discover from the Bible the sort of woman Dorcas was, and then try to deduce what might have been some of the reasons why God raised her to life. These clues will give us insights into the values upon which men and women will be judged worthy of the resurrection at the second advent. They will also pinpoint those character qualities which we ourselves will need to develop in our preparation for the glorious day.

Dorcas was called "a certain disciple" by Luke. Acts 9:36. This expression suggests that she was well known in her community of Christians. In this context a "disciple" is one who has accepted the discipline of the life and teachings of Christ. Matthew 25:35, 36. Is it possible that Dorcas herself had listened to His words "clothe the naked," or might she have been told of them by others? We shall never know. But carry them out she surely did! Dorcas, as a believer in the

Messiah, practiced her faith. In fact, in *The Acts of the Apostles,* page 131, we read that "she was a worthy disciple of Jesus, and her life was filled with acts of kindness." The first point which the historian makes is that Dorcas had accepted into her life the ideal qualities for which her Saviour stood and daily sought by God's grace to live in conformity with them to the best of her ability. By raising her to life the Lord endorsed her "works" of faith and love.

Luke focuses on two of her qualifications, explaining that Dorcas was "a woman . . . full of good works and almsdeeds which she did." Acts 9:36. Her "good works" were an outgrowth of her talents directed by her dedication to God. *The Acts of the Apostles* notes that "her skillful fingers were more active than her tongue." She had discovered her ability as a seamstress and had decided to employ her gifts to help those in need. She sought out the poor who required warm clothing and did her best to supply them. Her "good works" involved a personal commitment on her part. Too many Christians merely donate money and then feel that they have done their duty. Dorcas first gave of herself to the needy, and then each stitch she put into each garment was a part of her energies, her thought, her time, her skill, and herself.

Luke's added term "almsdeeds" grows from the root which means mercy, pity, or compassion. We might render it "acts of compassion" into which Dorcas put all the sympathy of her loving heart. She sensed the needs of the poor and sought to meet them by her gifts. In contrast with her "good works," which consisted of the production of garments, her "almsdeeds" or gifts of compassion, were added monetary donations or the sharing of items which had not cost her any personal effort to manufacture. Dorcas thus gave not only of herself and her talents but also of her possessions and resources. "Her life was filled with acts of kindness. She knew who needed comfortable clothing and who needed sympathy, and she freely ministered to the poor and the sorrowful."— *Ibid*.

The widows whom she had helped remembered specifically "the coats and garments which Dorcas made." Acts 9:39. The form of Luke's verb suggests that she was in the habit of making these clothes. This gives us a further glimpse into her heart. Her life's design was consistent and continuous. To make gifts of this kind, much careful thought and planning were needed. For coats and other garments to be worth while, they must fit the person for whom they are made and be suitable in color and style. To produce such valued presents Dorcas invested time in study and research of individual requirements. Every garment was a silent testimony of her concern and thought. She personally gave herself to the needy because she had given herself to Christ.

Besides her contributions to the well-being of the community Dorcas had been of great service to the church. Her selfless ministry to others had produced evangelistic results. Souls had accepted Christ as Saviour and Lord because of the witness of her life. For these reasons "God saw fit to bring her back from the land of the enemy, that her skill and energy might still be a blessing to others."—*Ibid*., p. 132. Observing how her dedicated life had helped His kingdom to grow and prosper, the Lord purposed that by her resurrection her deeds might be continued and her God adored and His kingdom strengthened. And this miraculous event became "known throughout all Joppa; and many believed in the Lord." Acts 9:42. Thus by her life, as well as by her death, and then by her resurrection, Dorcas enlarged and established the cause of God.

In all the details of the character and activities of Dorcas, there is no mention of her theology or doctrinal beliefs. Dorcas was brought back to life on the basis of her good deeds that are the evidence of saving faith in her life and experience. In His description of the last judgment, our Lord divided all mankind into classes, "sheep" and "goats," distinctly separate from each other. The sheep at His right hand were commended because of the good deeds they had performed, while the goats on His left were condemned on the basis of their lack of acceptable works. See Matthew 25:31-46.

While the Bible emphasizes that nothing which a sinner has done or can do procures his acceptance by God, it is equally true that once he has become a disciple, good deeds must be the outgrowth of his relationship with the Saviour. "Works" on the part of the Christian do not earn merit, but without works he cannot remain a disciple. The final verdict of the judgment is based, not upon theological beliefs or saving knowledge, but on what the candidate for heaven has done during his life. Solomon emphasized this point when he said, "God shall bring every work into judgment, with every secret thing, whether it be good, or whether it be evil" (Ecclesiastes 12:14), and upon these works eternal survival hangs. Resurrection to the life which has no end thus depends upon the good deeds—evidence of saving faith in the experience of a Christian—performed during this life through the empowering grace of the Holy Spirit.

Dorcas is a perfect example of the life of service which will result in the resurrection of a Christian. Initially she had become a disciple by her avowed personal decision to accept the teaching of Jesus and submit to His grace and mercy. Then her life of service, her good works, and her kindly thoughts gave evidence of her saving faith, and for this reason—plus the faith-filled prayers of the saints— she was raised to life by God through his human instrument. Another reason for this decision on the part of God was that her ministry was not yet complete.

Through the centuries Dorcas has been the inspiration for innumerable societies of kindly Christian sisters and brothers who have devoted their talents to the production of clothes and other items for the needy. Dorcas is a worthy illustration of the "sheep" on the right hand of the judging Saviour. Here is an interesting warning by Ellen G. White on the place of "good works." "Never leave the impression on the mind that there is little or nothing to do on the part of man; but rather teach man to cooperate with God, that he may be successful in overcoming.

"Let no one say that your works have nothing to do with your rank and position before God. In the judgment the sentence pronounced is according to what has been done or to what has been left undone."—*Selected Messages*, bk. 1, p. 381.

Dorcas was a sanctified woman, for "the righteousness of Christ [which] consists in right actions and good works from pure, unselfish motives" she possessed in rich measure.—*Testimonies*, vol. 3, p. 528. Each day, as well as in the judgment, "our characters are revealed by what we do. The works show whether the faith is genuine.

"It is not enough to believe the theory of truth. . . . Whatever our profession, it amounts to nothing unless Christ is revealed in works of righteousness."—*Christ's Object Lessons*, pp. 312, 313. Across the centuries the story of the resurrected Dorcas urges us to study the harmony which must exist between faith and works, and then by the grace of God to bring this duet into correct balance in our lives. Today, she "being dead yet speaketh." Let us heed her call to "good works" and "almsdeeds."

Caleb—Fearless Spy

Caleb is the most famous spy in all the Scriptures, but we might never have heard of him had not the crisis arisen among the Israelites at Kadesh-barnea. This town was only eleven days' march from Sinai and stood as the gateway leading to the Promised Land. From this place God purposed that the armies of Israel should attack the Canaanites awaiting them and conquer Palestine. At this juncture some among the people suggested to Moses that spies should be sent to reconnoiter the best route to follow in the battle campaign and ascertain the condition and deployment of the enemy. In other words they proposed doing a feasibility study. Numbers 13:1-20. Ellen White points out that "the matter was presented before the Lord by Moses, and permission was granted."—*Patriarchs and Prophets*, p. 387.

But the Lord had provided everything which Israel had needed since they left Egypt. By His cooling cloud and illuminating fire He had led His people safely along a path unknown to them up to this point and had supplied their every need. Why should anyone doubt that He would continue leading now? Was the recommendation of the people a suggestion that spies could find a better route to victory in the conquest of Canaan than could the Lord by His pillar of cloud and fire? Perhaps the Lord's acquiescence that they go ahead was a test for the leaders and for the children of Israel as well.

Among the twelve spies chosen was Caleb, the representative of the tribe of Judah. Caleb is called the son of Jephunneh, who is designated "the Kenezite." Joshua 14:14. As the process of the settlement progressed, the boundaries of Judah were specified. It was then that Joshua "gave him [Caleb] a part among the children of Judah, according to the commandment of the Lord to Joshua, the city of Arba the father of Anak, which city is Hebron." Joshua 15:13. These words strongly suggest that Caleb was an Israelite only by adoption. From consulting the public register we learn that Caleb is called the "son of Jephunneh" (1 Chronicles 4:15) and is also termed the head of his father's house and the uncle of Othniel. Judges 1:13. A scenario something like this fits the facts given in Scripture. A Kenite took service with Judah and went down to Egypt at the migration led by Jacob. He or his son married a daughter of Perez, and so eventually Caleb was born, who inherited the family prerogatives and eventually became the leader of Judah.

This foreigner had learned to love the Lord and had accepted His laws and covenant. He was then absorbed into the tribe of Judah, where he attained a place of power and influence because of his faith in God. Possessing ancient ties to a foreign country, a fact never quite forgotten in the Scriptures, Caleb learned to live the life of a true Israelite and served God and His people with quiet and trusting fidelity.

Have you wondered what kind of person would have been selected as a spy? He would need to be resourceful and fearless, adaptable and enterprising, and observant and cool in trying circumstances. He must also have been well-controlled and able to evaluate various situations before he calculated the odds. For forty days the dozen men secretly investigated the country of Palestine, and to their joy, discovered that the land had everything about it which they had been promised.

It was rich and fruitful, beautiful and inviting. But, alas, and here was the rub, it was peopled with giants. The warriors lived in cities with walls stretching up to the heavens. Numbers 13:26-29. When their task was completed all the twelve returned to the encampment bringing some of the best produce they had found. Numbers 13:23-25.

Learning of the arrival of the party of explorers, the people gathered about them in great excitement to hear their reports. Everyone was thrilled with the samples of fruit that had been brought back, as well as the description of the countryside. But as the Israelites listened in growing consternation to the depictions of the size of the children of Anak and the defenses of their cities, gladness gave way to despair. The more they talked, the more vehement the ten spies became. In fact, they talked themselves into the certainty that it was now impossible for Israel to occupy Palestine. And soon they had all the people of God actually lifting up their voices, weeping in frustration (Numbers 14:1) at the thought of the giants.

At this juncture Caleb's character emerges. Certain that the difficulties were being overemphasized by the discouraged spies and that the people were overreacting, he pressed himself before the multitude with his counter proposal. As a result "Caleb stilled the people before Moses, and said, Let us go up at once, and possess it; for we are well able to overcome it." Numbers 13:30. Caleb had read the mood of the crowd, and with the force of his personality and his charisma quieted their clamoring. Filled with faith in the promises of God and certain that His people could succeed in their divinely appointed enterprise with His help, this man of decision and promptness recommended starting immediately on their God-planned task. We can see that Caleb was not afraid to speak his mind, even though he might be in the minority. His motto was "If God gives a command, obey!"

But unfortunately the "giants" won out! All too soon disappointment gave way to frustration. This degenerated into anger and resentment. Soon someone actually recommended that a captain be elected to lead the lately emancipated twelve tribes of Israel back into their Egyptian slavery once more. Numbers 14:2-4; Nehemiah 9:17. While Moses and Aaron were on their knees beseeching the Lord for guidance, Caleb again "urged his way to the front, and his clear, ringing voice was heard above all the clamor of the multitude. He opposed the cowardly views of his fellow spies, which had weakened the faith and courage of all Israel," and he begged the people not to rebel against their Lord. See *Testimonies,* vol. 4, p. 149, and Numbers 14:5-9.

During this crisis Caleb emerged as the fearless advocate of what he considered to be the right course of action. He clearly "comprehended the situation, and, bold to stand in defense of the word of God, he did all in his power to counteract the evil influence of his unfaithful associates. . . . He did not contradict what had already been said; the walls were high and the Canaanites strong. But God had promised the land to Israel."—*Patriarchs and Prophets,* p. 388.

But now, in response, the ten spies united more vehemently in opposing Caleb's view, and soon the whole congregation became so incensed that they picked up rocks to stone Caleb and Joshua. They were restrained from carrying out their purpose only by the sudden appearance of the Shekinah at the tabernacle and the sentence which the Lord pronounced against them. Numbers 14:10-12. In the dark days which followed, the ten unfaithful spies perished, and in their execution the Israelites read their own fate and Caleb's reward. Read Numbers 14:20-24 and *Patriarchs and Prophets,* p. 391.

After the confusion and bitterness had subsided, the Lord explained his future purpose for Israel. None of that rebellious generation would ever enter Canaan.

Numbers 14:23, 29. Of His trusty representative the Lord declared, "My servant Caleb, because he had another spirit with him, and hath followed me fully, him will I bring into the land whereinto he went; and his seed shall possess it." Numbers 14:24. What a thrilling accolade! The Lord had observed that Caleb had followed His instructions fully. "It was Caleb's faith in God that gave him courage; that kept him from the fear of man, even the mighty giants, the sons of Anak, and enabled him to stand boldly and unflinchingly in defense of the right."—*Testimonies,* vol. 5, p. 378.

"Caleb was faithful and steadfast. He was not boastful, he made no parade of his merits and good deeds; but his influence was always on the side of right."— *Ibid,* p. 303. And for thirty-eight years, while individuals of that generation of rebels one by one fell in the desert, Caleb patiently and uncomplainingly remained steadfast among the diminishing survivors, looking forward to the fulfillment of God's promises to him individually and to His people as a whole.

For the thirty-eight years of wandering in the wilderness, Caleb marched with death as his daily companion. Having watched his peers perish one by one for their rebellion, he found himself at last once more at Kadesh-barnea. What memories must have crowded his mind! Israel had come back to the place from which the previous generation had turned away from God. The young people were now confronted with the same choices which their fathers had faced. The land was still beautiful and fruitful. The next generation of giants in their walled cities were still poised, waiting, now even bolder and more defiant against God and His people than they had been previously. But the Lord was still leading those who chose to follow. Caleb must have remembered with regret what had gone on at the spot so many years before, actions that had proved themselves to be so useless, so destructive. But his own courage had grown stronger than ever through the passing decades. Although eighty-five years old, he was still ready to start immediately to take possession of the land; and with the new generation of young people, he did just that. And God fulfilled every promise He had made to Caleb (Numbers 14:30; 32:11, 12; Deuteronomy 1:36), and although their peers had perished, Joshua and Caleb still lived and triumphed gloriously.

Victory followed victory as Israel advanced under God's leadership, and the time soon came to divide up the land between the tribes. At this juncture, with the other chiefs of the tribe of Judah, Caleb made an eloquent appeal to Joshua. He reminded the successor of Moses, who was now the chieftain of God's people, of the Lord's promise to him. He reiterated to Joshua, who had once been his fellow explorer, all that had transpired at Kadesh-barnea long before, when he had "wholly followed the Lord." Joshua 14:8. God had through Moses then assured him and his children that the portion of the land he had himself explored as a spy would one day be theirs. He then asked Joshua for a birthday present! "I am this day fourscore and five years old," he said, and claiming God's promises, said, "I am as strong this day as I was in the day that Moses sent me. . . . Now therefore give me this mountain. . . . If . . . the Lord . . . be with me, then I shall be able to drive them out." Joshua 14:10-12. Caleb's power in God did not diminish through age. The difficult terrain he requested was the home of the very giants whose presence had so discouraged Israel almost forty-five years before. Caleb now longed to validate the Lord's promise that His people would be empowered to drive the enemy out. He well knew that problems do not disappear, but he knew better than ever that the Lord gives solutions to them all.

The sequel to his request was that "Caleb drove thence the three sons of Anak." Joshua 15:14. He realized why he was in Canaan clearly because he comprehended God's plan for Israel and himself. His faith and action sprang from the fact that he apprehended that for which he had been apprehended by God. Philippians 3:12. Had Israel listened to him in the first place, this conquest would have taken place decades earlier, and the history of millions of persons would have been so different. Strong, independent, fearless, totally trusting in God's promises, "Calebs are the men most needed in these last days."—*Ibid.*, p. 130.

The aged Caleb showed himself also to be a motivator of good men. He now planned for a brave and resourceful husband for his daughter. To discover such a man he issued a challenge to his soldiers. The man who would capture the heights of Hebron, the very stronghold of the most powerful of the enemy, should receive the hand of his daughter in marriage. Joshua 15:13-16. Othniel took up this challenge, and by God's aid won both the fortress and his bride. So perceptive did Caleb's judgment of character prove, that Othniel later became a successful judge in Israel. Joshua 15:17; Judges 1:13; 3:9.

Emboldened by her father's personal request to Joshua for Hebron, Caleb's daughter Achsah came forward with a petition of her own. Would her father give her an inheritance too? And while in those far off days only sons normally received patrimonies, Caleb, independent and generous, granted her the property she had chosen and which was watered by the springs she had desired. Joshua 15:16-19.

God's estimate of Caleb is condensed in these words: Caleb had followed the Lord's will "wholly" (Numbers 32:12; Joshua 14:8, 9, 14) and "fully" (Numbers 14:24). And as he had served his God, so God rewarded him.

Caleb is a shining example of what God wants of his leaders in all ages. "While the doubting ones talk of impossibilities, while they tremble at the thought of high walls and strong giants, let the faithful Calebs, who have 'another spirit,' come to the front."—*Ibid.*,

p. 380. The Holy Spirit dwelt in his heart and made the assurances and promises of God, which to some of his peers were theoretical and out-of-date, vital and dynamic in his life. Caleb did not move from impulse, but carefully weighed the situation in the light of heaven. He came to understand the true nature of the conditions he met, and grew to be one of the most perceptive spies. Even though misunderstood and condemned by the majority of his companions, Caleb looked upon the problems from God's point of view. He thoroughly believed that God had the solutions, as well as the power to carry them through.

Caleb had originally been chosen by his peers for his role as a spy because he was a recognized leader of merit. Later, when his opinions crossed those of the emotional mob and they threatened him with stoning, he still remained independent and steadfast to his purpose. "We want Calebs now who will press to the front—chieftains in Israel who with courageous words will make a strong report in favor of immediate action. When the selfish, ease-loving, panic-stricken people, fearing tall giants and inaccessible walls, clamor for retreat, let the voice of the Calebs be heard, even though the cowardly ones stand with stones in their hands, ready to beat them down for their faithful testimony."—*Testimonies,* p. 383. Men of this caliber "are salt that retains the savor," writes Mrs. White in the same volume, page 130.

This child of strangers, this adopted son of Israel, this elected spy of Canaan, this prince of the house of Judah, this spokesman of God and encourager of His people, faithfully, steadfastly, fully followed on to know his Lord, seeing and implicitly obeying the will of his Master. Such leaders are needed today to blaze the trail for the faithful ones on their way to the kingdom of heaven. The church needs such men to encourage others to follow the light with zeal unflagging and enthusiasm unabated even into life's old age.

Miriam—Forgiven Sister

The Scriptures introduce Miriam shyly, coyly, bravely, emerging from the bushes, to carry out one of the most important tasks in the history of the world. From her hiding place she had watched over the little ark of rushes in which her baby brother lay asleep, among the reeds about the Nile. This helpless babe was destined to grow into the greatest legislator who ever lived, a man whose writings still mold the minds of men. Miriam had helped her mother prepare the tiny craft and its precious cargo for a journey on the Nile and into the unknown future. And then this young girl had stood guard, waiting. She had probably not even thought through what she would say and what was expected of her. But when the Egyptian princess looked sympathetically at the innocent crying baby and read the story of his life, Miriam recognized the princess' sympathy and intuitively was ready with the correct suggestion. "Shall I go and call to thee a nurse of the Hebrew women, that she may nurse the child for thee?" (Exodus 2:7), the little girl asked.

What a witty child Moses' sister proved to be! And when the answer was Yes, I can see her skipping off to fetch her mother with her exciting piece of news. In this adventure Miriam's personality shines out clearly. Ellen White perceptively observed that "Miriam's force of character had been early displayed when as a child she watched beside the Nile the little basket in which was hidden the infant Moses. Her self-control and tact God had made instrumental in preserving the deliverer of His people."—*Patriarchs and Prophets,* p. 382.

The Scriptures are silent regarding Miriam for the next eighty years. Her brother Moses grew to manhood, became the general of the world's most powerful army, refused to accept the throne of Egypt, and by an act of foolhardy bravado exiled himself to the land of Midian. During his forty years of absence from Egypt conditions for the Israelites had gone from bad to worse. Cringing in terror from the taskmaster's lash, the Hebrews hoped against hope for the promised deliverer to appear. And then dramatically and unexpectedly Moses was back in Egypt. Soon it was Pharaoh's turn to cower beneath the ten strokes of divine retribution. Then there followed in quick succession the hasty Paschal meal, the midnight flight from Egypt, the stupendous happenings at the Red Sea, which left the hosts of Pharaoh washed up on the shore, and Israel standing triumphant, basking in the smile of God, free at last and hopeful for the future.

The contrast between the hopeless bondsmen gazing in abject terror at the advancing chariots of Egypt and the unexpected and dramatic act of divine deliverance lifted the Israelites' spirits into an ecstasy of joy which could find expression only in poetry and song. "The Spirit of God rested upon Moses, and he led the people in a triumphant anthem of thanksgiving, the earliest and one of the most sublime that are known to man." See Exodus 15:1-18.

"Like the voice of the great deep, rose from the vast hosts of Israel that sublime ascription. It was taken up by the women of Israel, Miriam, the sister of Moses, leading the way, as they went forth with timbrel and dance. Far over desert and sea rang the joyous refrain, and the mountains re-echoed the words of their praise—'Sing ye to Jehovah, for He hath triumphed gloriously.' "—*Ibid.*, pp. 288, 289.

In this scene by the Red Sea we see Miriam again. By this time she is a respected and acknowledged prophetess ninety-two years old. Her charisma and vitality enable her to lead the vast throng of Israelite women in an antiphonal response to the hymn of praise lifted heavenward by the Hebrew men led by her brother Moses. I like to imagine Miriam advancing before the hosts of God as they began their march to Sinai, "with timbrel and dance," not with twirling baton, prancing, vulgar step, and suggestive gesture, but in solemn joy and heartfelt praise for a victory wholly provided by God.

In what circumstances and upon what conditions Miriam had been called to join her brothers, Moses and Aaron, in the government of Israel we are not told. Inspiration simply notes that "Aaron and Miriam had occupied a position of high honor and leadership in Israel. Both were endowed with the prophetic gift, and both had been divinely associated with Moses in the deliverance of the Hebrews. 'I sent before thee Moses, Aaron, and Miriam' (Micah 6:4), are the words of the Lord by the prophet Micah."—*Ibid.*, p. 382. Among the three children of Amram and Jochebed who had attained positions of summit leadership in Israel, the prophetess Miriam was equally recognized as divinely called and appointed. Had it not been for the marriage of Moses, Miriam would have been a sovereign woman in Israel to the day of her death.

While in exile Moses had married a woman of Midian, "a descendant of Abraham. In personal appearance she differed from the Hebrews in being of a somewhat darker complexion. Though not an Israelite, Zipporah was a worshiper of the true God. She was of a timid, retiring disposition, gentle and affectionate, and greatly distressed at the sight of suffering; and it was for this reason that Moses, when on the way to

Egypt, had consented to her return to Midian. He desired to spare her the pain of witnessing the judgments that were to fall on the Egyptians."—*Ibid.*, pp. 383, 384.

During the absence of Zipporah, while history was being made for Israel in Egypt and beyond, Miriam had held the ear of Moses and, with her brother Aaron, had led in the policy-making decisions of God's people. But when Israel approached Sinai, Moses requested his father-in-law to bring Zipporah and their two sons to the encampment.

On his arrival the observant Jethro immediately saw that Moses was trying to accomplish the impossible. He advised his son-in-law to divide his many responsibilities of leadership among trusted administrators. This counsel Moses recognized as timely and invaluable, and immediately and readily accepted. See Exodus 18:13-26.

Later on, when Moses was again overworked, he complained to the Lord that he was "not able to bear all this people alone." Numbers 11:14. This time the Lord told him to choose seventy elders and promised Moses that they would "bear the burden of the people" with him. Verse 17. In his appointment of the seventy elders, however, Moses did not consult with Aaron and Miriam. Because of this continued seeming neglect, they grew jealous that their authority had been divided among others. This resentment was fueled by the fact that their brother had earlier accepted the advice of a foreigner, a despised Midianite, and had apparently slighted them. All this "aroused in Aaron and Miriam a fear that his influence with the great leader exceeded theirs."—*Ibid.*, p. 383. A further factor which stirred up the envy of Miriam and Aaron was the organization of the council of leaders. Because of the powers vested in this body "they felt that their position and authority had been ignored." —*Ibid*.

Miriam and Aaron, while the associates of Moses

97

and sharing his authority, had never really shared in bearing the burdens of leadership. Advice is cheap, but responsibility to act is too often shunned. They had failed to discern the enormous amount of work which Moses was attempting alone, and because of their vested interest in their positions, they refused to agree to the wisdom of appointing any further directors. They regarded themselves as being equally honored by God as was Moses and began to criticize him and to question among themselves the way in which he exercised his authority in these arrogant words, "Hath the Lord indeed spoken only by Moses? hath he not spoken also by us?" Numbers 12:2.

Miriam found still another cause of complaint against her brother in her sister-in-law. She disapproved of his marriage. "That he should choose a woman of another nation, instead of taking a wife from among the Hebrews, was an offense to her family and national pride. Zipporah was treated with ill-disguised contempt."—*Ibid.*, p. 383. Miriam felt that she was being ignored. "Here was the chief reason for Miriam's antipathy to Zipporah," continues Mrs. White in *Patriarchs and Prophets,* page 384. "Smarting under the supposed neglect shown to herself and Aaron, she regarded the wife of Moses as the cause, concluding that her influence had prevented him from taking them into his counsels as formerly." At this juncture Miriam set about turning her brother Aaron against Moses and his leadership.

At the crisis of this family quarrel, precipitated by envy and racism, the Lord summoned Moses and Aaron and Miriam to the tabernacle, and there denounced Miriam and Aaron for talking against His appointed leader. " 'And the anger of the Lord was kindled against them; and He departed.' The cloud disappeared from the tabernacle in token of God's displeasure, and Miriam was smitten. She 'became leprous, white as snow.' Aaron was spared, but he was severely rebuked in Miriam's punishment.''—*Ibid.*, p. 385.

Moses the lawgiver, Aaron the high priest, and the seventy elders, together with all Israel, looked on with terror as Miriam was struck with leprosy. All must have staggered back in horror at the sight. Then the Lord pronounced sentence against Miriam. Driven from the camp for seven days by order from Heaven, Miriam was the object lesson of God's disapproval of the sins of slander and calumny. Compelled to cry "Unclean! Unclean!" kept away from the homes of men, living alone in the wilderness, Miriam had time to reflect on her sinful conduct. Today we are to see God's judgment on envy in His treatment of Miriam. With flesh half consumed by her disease, with voice cracked and hoarse, Miriam was loathsome and loathed. Yahweh dramatically displayed in her what would be the results to those who revolted against His appointees and sinned in maligning God's leaders. They are dead while seeming alive.

What an incredible week that must have been for the hosts of Israel! Millions of men and women, on their way to the Promised Land, halted in their tracks by the results of the attitude and words of one envy-wracked woman! Do you think that it was a small matter for a sister to criticize her brother and despise her sister-in-law? Read God's attitude clearly written in Miriam's leprosy. Then, in answer to the prayers of Moses, Miriam was cleansed and allowed back into camp, chastised and humbled, no longer a "seditious whisperer." Note the effects of rebellion on one who had been endowed with the gift of prophecy. In vain we search in the Scriptures for Miriam's later rulership role. Because of her conduct she ruined her influence as a prophetess and ceased to be a leader of Israel. In the later sacred story she is completely ignored.

For thirty-eight years the people of God continued their steady and benumbing march into death. Each year the number of survivors lessened. Moses and Aaron were still the leaders, but Miriam's influence for good is conspicuous by its absence. In the fortieth year after the hosts of God had left Egypt, the three children of Amram and Jochebed faced the inevitable end of their life's journey. Aaron, weak and pliable at the time of the making of the golden calf, had grown strong in the Lord, but in the judgment of God he must still die at Mount Hor. Moses, unparalleled in history as a leader and organizer and legislator, because he had spoken unadvisedly with his lips must also die without entering the Promised Land. Concerning Miriam we are simply told that she "died." Numbers 20:1. One reaches the close of her career with a sense of sadness and regret. The rosy promise of the beginning and the successful blossoming of the middle are not matched by the fruit of the ending. Her brother Moses in his farewell address reminded Israel of the folly of rejecting divine leadership. He could think of no better illustration of this than his sister. His words are almost chilling, "Remember what the Lord thy God did unto Miriam by the way." Deuteronomy 24:9. Leprosy, the most dreaded of all diseases in Bible times, had been inflicted upon Miriam to signal God's estimate of criticism, envy, and backbiting, even of members of one's own family.

There is little doubt but that Miriam will one day reach God's Promised Land which lies beyond the grave. But with what regret must she have viewed her uncalled for conduct from the clear perspective of the end of her journey. Talents, poetry, music, charisma, the prophetic gift, humor, tact, and strength of character were all sacrificed on the altar of envy by the sword of her jealous tongue. Forgiven at least, by the mercy of God and the generosity of Moses and Zipporah, and with a face drenched with tears looking beyond the shadows toward the pearly gates, Miriam calls to us across the centuries, "Remember—"

Jonathan—Loyal Son and Friend

Jonathan, the eldest son of Israel's first king, by every norm of assessment, stands among the noblest persons in all of history. As crown prince of Israel he must have cherished for a time the prospect of succeeding his father to the throne. His tragic and yet triumphant life, as recorded in Scripture, falls naturally into three divisions. The first covers his relationship to his father, who, in spite of the Lord's disapproval of certain acts (1 Samuel 8:6-22), was, for a short time, the loved and respected king of God's chosen people. The second describes his relationship to the same king, finally rejected by God and slowly growing mad as he sold himself to the devil. The conclusion deals with his relationship to David, his rival to the throne. Through all these circumstances Jonathan never sought his own advantage nor complained that fate was cheating or misusing him. Loyalty to God, as well as to the Lord's chosen leaders, was the driving characteristic of his life.

Jonathan is introduced to us as the commander of one third of the army of God's people stationed at Gibeah to thwart the Philistine incursions. At this time his father, with two thousand troops, stood guard before Michmash. 1 Samuel 13:2. In this stalemate Jonathan was the first to obtain a breakthrough. With incredible personal bravery he "smote the garrison of the Philistines." Verse 3. The translation of the Hebrew word as "garrison" is misleading to us because the term really suggests a flagpole and indicates that a group of the enemy was stationed in that place. The same Hebrew word also describes Lot's wife, who became a "pillar" of salt, a monument of her materialism. Genesis 19:26; cf. 1 Samuel 10:5; 13:3, 4; 2 Samuel 8:6, 14; 2 Chronicles 8:10. The word is rendered "officers" and may be thought of as deputies; 17:2; 1 Kings 4:7, 19, ("officers" here may be thought of as overseers). What the prince actually did was to destroy the hated symbol of the rallying point of the Philistine presence and scatter his adversaries.

Jonathan's daring exploit electrified the people and encouraged the king, his father, to take the initiative in making a call for a general mobilization. 1 Samuel 13:3, 4. But Saul was a thoughtless leader, "and all the people followed him trembling." 1 Samuel 13:7. Some time earlier Samuel had given a directive to the king to do his part in preparing for war and then to wait for seven days. The prophet promised to come to consecrate the campaign with burnt and peace offerings to the Lord. 1 Samuel 10:8. But before the expiration of this time the impatient Saul, fearing the mood of his men, took matters into his own hands and illegally and blasphemously officiated at the altar himself. Knowing that this service should be performed by the priest alone (Numbers 3:10; 18:1-5, 8, 9; 16:40), Saul in this way brazenly demonstrated his defiance of God's mandate (1 Samuel 13:9).

On his arrival at the scene, even while the service was in progress, Samuel was horror-struck, and with broken heart predicted, "Now thy kingdom shall not continue: the Lord hath sought him a man after his own heart, and the Lord hath commanded him to be captain over his people." 1 Samuel 13:14. Here was the first intimation that someone outside Saul's family line would be chosen by the Lord to be the next king of

Israel. In these dread words Jonathan heard the death knell to his hopes of one day sitting upon his father's throne. And when the man of God left, ominous forbodings of disaster sapped the will of the Israelite soldiers to fight. The armies still stood indecisively facing each other, with Israel's morale rapidly deteriorating and their numbers dwindling through desertion.

"Now it came to pass upon a day, that Jonathan the son of Saul said unto the young man that bear his armour, Come, and let us go over to the Philistines' garrison." 1 Samuel 14:1. In this passage "garrison" is the rendering of a different word (from that which we noticed was found in 1 Samuel 13:3), and suggests entrenched forces. Ellen White has added this insight concerning Jonathan. "The king's son, a man who feared the Lord, was chosen as the instrument to deliver Israel. Moved by a divine impulse, he proposed to his armor-bearer that they should make secret attack upon the enemy's camp. 'It may be,' he urged, 'that the Lord will work for us: for there is no restraint to the Lord to save by many or by few.' "—*Patriarchs and Prophets*, p. 623. What courage! What faith! What leadership!

Among his talents Jonathan was an excellent judge of character. For his lifelong and closest friend he chose David, one of the greatest men of God of all time. And as his daily companion he selected an "armor-bearer, who was a man of faith and prayer."—*Ibid*. Stealthily the two men crept to within hailing distance of the enemy sentinels, and when Jonathan and his armor-bearer exposed themselves, they were soon discovered by the Philistine watchmen. In their prayer the two servants of God had agreed that should the enemy order them to remain where they were, they would do so; but if invited up into the Philistine encampment, they would take this to be a signal that God guaranteed them a victory.

At the contemptuous Philistine call, "Come up to

us, and we will shew you a thing," Jonathan whispered to his armor-bearer, "Come up after me: for the Lord hath delivered them into the hand of Israel." 1 Samuel 14:12. Crediting the success to God's power alone, the young prince fearlessly led his attacking force of one into the heart of the Philistine army. "Angels of heaven shielded Jonathan and his attendant, angels fought by their side."—*Ibid.*, p. 623. The Lord of hosts so confused the enemy soldiers that in the melee they actually started slaughtering one another. Saul and his soldiers, joined by the Israelite deserters who had been hiding in caves and thickets, now rallied to the kill. God frightened the confused Philistines by thundering from heaven and shaking the mountain with an earthquake, terrifying them into a rout; and thus a signal victory was won.

Hoping to instill discipline into his troops, the impetuous Saul had rashly forbidden them to partake of any food during the day. Ignorant of his father's ill-advised prohibition, Jonathan had refreshed himself during the battle by eating some honey dripping from a full comb in a tree he had passed. The soldiers who saw him do this, aware of the prince's breach of his father's anathema and afraid of the foreboding of doom which this pressaged, were unhappy and restive even in their triumph. Sensing that something was amiss, Saul consulted a priest, dressed with the Urim and Thummim, or sacred oracles, to try to discover the reason for the possible divine displeasure. The king put himself under oath that should guilt be found in anyone, including himself or his son, the culprit should be put to death immediately. By the determining lot Jonathan was identified as the offender and confessed his "crime." His father forthwith sentenced him to death. But the army soldiers rallying around the king's son, their prince, through whose gallantry the day's victory had been gained, angrily refused to permit the king to execute his son, and the matter was wisely, if sullenly, dropped by Saul. 1 Samuel 14:13-45.

Throughout this weird episode Jonathan stood amid the conflicts as a man in perfect control of himself, trusting his God implicitly, yet remaining a totally loyal soldier and son to his father and commander-in-chief. When told of Saul's curse, he responded mildly, "My father hath troubled the land." 1 Samuel 14:29. Later when condemned to death, he commented wistfully, "I did but taste a little honey with the end of the rod that was in mine hand, and, lo, I must die." 1 Samuel 14:43. He did not rail against his self-willed irrational king, nor make a self-pitying plea for mercy to the troops. Calm and unafraid, he faced death tranquilly, knowing that his times were in God's hands. That memorable day had begun as one of the most thrilling in Jonathan's life. His attack on the Philistine stronghold is perhaps the most gallant ever undertaken in the annals of war; and God had honored his faith and bravery. The day ended with an act of fortitude never seen in history. The acclaimed victor, without rallying in his own defense placidly awaited his death at the hand of an irrational and bigoted general, who happened to be his father. But the soldiers who had followed him to triumph would defend him to the last man.

One wonders at the role Jonathan played in face of the strutting and obscene Goliath. He evidently remained silent, afraid, uncertain, while Israel's king and Israel's soldiers listened, ashamed and sullen, to the pagan's daily taunts against their army and his blasphemy against their God. Then Jonathan must have watched in shocked amazement as a shepherd lad, with sling and stones, cut down the adversary and immediately led Israel to triumph over the Philistines. Jonathan, a master at discerning character quality, recognized at once the valuable traits possessed by David, and from that moment the two so different men became lifelong friends.

Because of Saul's disregard of the divine mandate to exterminate Amalek, Samuel again notified the king that God had in fact transferred his crown to another. 1 Samuel 15:1-31. Yet Saul refused to resign. When it became known to all that David had actually been anointed to be the next king, Saul resolved to do all in his power to murder his appointed successor. For the rest of his troubled life the king expended most of his thought and energies to this end. His son Jonathan, aware of the deteriorating relationship between Saul and Samuel, realized that this reflected a worsening relationship between his father and his God. During these years there were periods in which Saul accepted David into his home and court as friend and retainer, as well as son-in-law. 1 Samuel 18:27. But on other occasions an insane and violent fury flared up against David, as well as Jonathan, and Saul personally attempted to take their lives. At these times Jonathan "made intercession for his friend."—*Ibid.*, p. 655. In fact "the friendship of Jonathan for David was also of God's providence, to preserve the life of the future ruler of Israel."—*Ibid.*, p. 649. Is it not ironic that the heir apparent to Israel's throne should have been chosen by Heaven to ensure that God's man, David, should survive the attempts made against his life by King Saul in order that he might become the next king?

From the day he first met David, Jonathan loved and appreciated him, and the regard was mutual. 1 Samuel 18:1, 3; 19:2; 20:17; 2 Samuel 1:26. While Saul's hatred against David intensified, friendship strengthened between David and Saul's son. Saul grew more and more demented, until by his visit to the witch of Endor he sold himself to the devil. Through these dark years, Jonathan watched the course of his father and often remonstrated with him, all the while remaining loyal to him as his king. As David's star ascended, Jonathan's affection for the young man deepened. Jonathan's words at one separation were, "Go in peace. . . . The Lord be between me and thee, and between my seed and thy seed for ever" (1 Samuel 20:42), cadences evocative of a continuing relationship for which he longed and which he sensed could never be.

As we review the life of Jonathan, we watch in admiration his first recorded symbolic act, the removal of the tokens of his office—his robe and sword—and their presentation to David, his rival. 1 Samuel 18:4. Sensing that the son of Jesse was to be the next ruler of Israel, Jonathan thus stripped off his robe, his royal garments, even his sword and his bow and girdle as the symbols of his position and prerogative. This gesture was a well-known one in Israel. His father Saul had earlier laid aside his outer garments which typified his rank when he appeared merely as a common man before Samuel the prophet.—*Ibid.*, p. 654.

We listen in appreciation and admiration to the terms of Jonathan's covenant of friendship with the future king, in which he asks only for protection for his family when dynastic changes take place. 1 Samuel 20:8, 16, 17, 42; 23:18; 2 Samuel 21:7. We observe in satisfaction his thwarting of the plans of his father to assassinate David (1 Samuel 20:1-42; 23:16-18), when no one would have gained more by David's murder than he. It is recorded that "Jonathan spake good of David." 1 Samuel 19:4. And when the future king of Israel was discouraged, "Saul's son arose, and went to David into the wood, and strengthened his hand in God." 1 Samuel 23:16. Jonathan knew the Source of all true strength from personal experience. What a man! What a friend! What a Christian!

Shortly after Saul's Endor encounter with the devil through the witch, Israel was forced to join battle with the combined forces of Philistia. In the ensuing defeat of God's people, which Saul's disobedience and distraction precipitated, Jonathan vainly and loyally fought by his father's side until the end.

Throughout his life Jonathan had submitted to God's will wherever it might lead. His loyalty to his divinely appointed leaders—Samuel the prophet, Saul the king, and David, the anointed heir to the throne—is amazing. We, too, sometimes encounter officials in church and in society whose relationships with God and their fellows are unhealthy and whose performance in office is poor, and we make this an excuse to criticize and condemn them. As Christians, however, we should submit to the "powers that be" (Romans 13:1; also see verses 2-7 and Daniel 4:17) without complaining insofar as our consciences are not violated (Acts 5:29). And we should support to the best of our abilities the elected leaders of our country and our church, irrespective of our personal ambitions.

The meek and wise-hearted, the loving and loyal Jonathan smiles across the centuries assuring us that his faithfulness to the rejected king was endorsed by God, even though it ended at the point of a Philistine spear. Refusing to fight for an earthly throne and a jeweled crown which he might have claimed, he happily yielded both to a divinely chosen rival whom he loved and supported, and thus gained at last an eternal throne and the crown of everlasting life.

Courageous, magnanimous, totally lacking jealousy and guile, he was utterly sincere and richly pious. A search of the pages of worldwide biography fails to reveal a story of friendship comparable with that which existed between Jonathan, the crown prince of Israel, and David, the divinely annointed heir, who was his rival to the throne. True friendship is a rare boon. To be linked with the same life at 40 as at 14, to understand and be understood, to share one's fears and hopes and not feel vulnerable, these are qualities of the friendship which the selfless Jonathan established. His love for David is the most self-effacing and self-renouncing affection the world has seen, apart from Christ's love for His enemies.

Who in the long story of human folly has been faced with the conflict of interests which confronted Jonathan, and who has resolved them better? Loyalty to an insane, bigoted and godless father was delicately balanced against friendship with a man who was his rival and the enemy of the king. And in the judgment of earth Jonathan emerges only to be struck down by a Philistine spear, unsaluted and untriumphant. Resting in some unmarked tomb, the greatest friend of the Old Testament reflected the affection and concern of Him whose empty tomb proclaims that His friendship "sticketh closer than a brother" (Proverbs 18:24), nearer than thought or breath, and ready to help us now.

You wonder if — just possibly — Jonathan was one of the First Fruits @ the Crucifixion!

Epilogue

We have come to the end of our study of some of the men and women in the Scriptures who were victors. They were mostly very ordinary and comparatively unimportant people, yet in their own ways they were unique, and certainly singled out by God for special favors. Their feelings and ambitions were just like ours. Their sins and weaknesses mirror our own. Their emotional needs were similar to those which we ourselves have. The circumstances which called forth their efforts to serve the Lord in some special way were not more dramatic than those which we encounter, and the events which brought about their descent into sin occur in our daily lives all too often.

Frustration in the face of a stupid husband or discord caused by a jealous and vindictive sister are common enough. The need to face life when someone has been appointed to the job we have held or has been chosen as our successor in a career from which we are thwarted from continuing occurs daily. Yet these were the conditions in which and through which the saints we have studied gained the right to be called victors. The problems they solved are still common problems challenging us today.

The questions we have constantly asked ourselves in our study is this: Why were they able to triumph, while others failed miserably? The answer to this question is the answer to life's greatest quest. All who triumphed refused to think of themselves as great or successful. Some of them did, of course, before they overcame. Pride, self-will, stubbornness were the factors which tripped them up. But once these had been recognized and by the grace of God eradicated from their lives, the road was open to victory through the guidance of the Spirit.

A recognition of the time and the circumstances in which life's watersheds occur in the experiences of others is most important. To recognize David's threat to Saul, to sense the import of Samuel's anointing of David, to grasp the change in the attitude to Saul of Tarsus, and the necessity for Dorcas to continue her ministry, these insights came only through the power of the Spirit. To seize the opportunity Providence presents to do something for our fellowmen or for the cause of God is vital, and this drive, too, needs the guiding light.

Each one of these persons we have studied had his own kind of needs and his own supply of help, which the Lord provided as required. But the problems which these men and women faced were not theoretical or theological. They were not involved with the meaning of recondite ideas, but with the solution of practical problems. This does not mean that beliefs regarding God and His will are unimportant, or that these persons were ignorant of the relationships which must exist between them and God. Their understandings of the divine outworkings were clear and abiding. But they were all involved in what should be done, within the parameters of Heaven's sanctions, to bless men and glorify God, and each in his or her own ways eventually succeeded.

This leads us to a consideration of how we should apply these biblical stories to our lives. On our knees we should seek to understand our own problems and personal needs. By close scrutiny and self-examination we should discover the areas in which we need to over-come. Then, instead of blaming relations, friends, enemies, or circumstances for our conditions, we should seek for divine power to solve our problems, enheartened by these examples of men and women who were victors before us. Since they were enabled to triumph, we also may be. The same God reigns. The same devil is a thousand-times-over defeated foe. The same circumstances are around us to be used as means to success rather than as factors which spell defeat. These victors have blazed the trail for us. Let us joyfully, hopefully, trustingly follow after the same Leader who guided their pathway into light.

The same Jesus who has helped in every age and every circumstance says to us, "Lo, I am with you alway, even unto the end of the world." Take His hand in yours, and walk with Him until He places on your head the crown of victory.